# A Slice of Cherry Pie

For Rob and for Mum, with all my love.

In loving memory of my sister Miriam; the wind beneath my wings.

# A Slice of Cherry Pie

## Julia Parsons

Absolute Press

First published in Great Britain
in 2010 by
**Absolute Press**
Scarborough House
29 James Street West
Bath BA1 2BT
*Phone* 44 (0) 1225 316013
*Fax* 44 (0) 1225 445836
*E-mail* info@absolutepress.co.uk
*Website* www.absolutepress.co.uk

Text copyright
© Julia Parsons, 2010
This edition copyright
© Absolute Press
Food Photography copyright
© Cristian Barnett

**Publisher** Jon Croft
**Commissioning Editor**
Meg Avent
**Editor** Jane Bamforth
**Design** Matt Inwood
and Claire Siggery
**Photographer** Cristian Barnett
**Food Styling** Andrea O'Connor

ISBN 13: 9781906650278
Printed and bound in Slovenia on
behalf of Latitude Press

**A note about the text**
This book was set using Century.
The first Century typeface was cut
in 1894. In 1975 an updated family
of Century typefaces was designed
by Tony Stan for ITC.

6 Introduction
9 Cook's notes

11 Cherry blossom
33 Sunshine and lemons
57 Poppy fields
71 Pebbles and ice cream
99 Linen and tea roses
119 Rain on glass
145 Wood smoke and roasts
171 Snow flurries

200 Index
205 Credits
206 Some things about me
207 A note for American
    readers
208 Thank you

*Food is at the heart and soul of life.* Not only does it give us the vital nourishment we need to live and breathe, but it also gives us great enjoyment and sensory pleasure. Food can soothe, comfort, awaken and enliven, and it has the ability to stimulate all of our senses, having a lasting effect on our emotions and our memories. It forms an important part of our family and social lives, our history and our culture.
The way we source it, the way we cook it, the way we eat it, tells so much about who we are and the lives we lead.

My love affair with food started fairly late and blossomed when I moved out of my parents' house and started cooking for myself. The food I'd grown up with was honest, hearty English food, designed to feed a family on a small budget. It was good and homely, traditional and somewhat reserved. When I eventually flew the nest, armed with a couple of cookbooks and an inquisitive appetite, I began to buy and cook with unfamiliar ingredients, embarking upon an exciting and liberating culinary voyage of discovery. Back then I had no idea just how far it would take me or how completely and passionately I would embrace it.

My first home of my own, for just my two little dogs and me, was a rented two-bedroom terrace house. It was tiny and narrow, sandwiched between two other houses, but that didn't matter; it was my home, my retreat safe from the world, to nest down in and to throw wide open to my friends and family. I loved dressing it up with candles and flowers, cushions and throws, and what I loved the most was entertaining and cooking for the people I loved. But I had a lot to learn and so I turned to books and television for my culinary education.

Once I started trying new ingredients and experiencing new flavours I couldn't get enough and with wide eyes and eager taste buds I took it all in. I discovered the vibrant and aromatic world of herbs and spices, an array of oils and vinegars, cuts of meat I'd never heard of and different types of sugar which, up until then, I had thought only came in white, brown and icing. Everything was fresh and exciting and the more I learned the more I wanted to learn. As I grew braver and more adventurous I bought game and seafood to cook at home, looking up what to do with it in my by now growing pile of cookbooks. I started adjusting recipes to my own taste and to the ingredients I had in the fridge, making notes as I went along.

When I got connected to the internet my interest in cooking was taken to a whole new level. I suddenly had access to an immensely vast, and continuously growing, source of information quite literally at my fingertips, and I could talk to people all over the world about what food they were buying, cooking and eating. I started experimenting more, trying different flavour combinations, relying less on the cookbooks and more on my instinct.

I discovered the world of food blogs back in 2006 and I knew straight away that this would be the perfect outlet for the passion I'd found, and so I started my own blog, www.asliceofcherrypie.com. In the beginning I had only a handful of readers – mostly friends and family – but as I kept at it I started to build up a regular readership. I loved the fact that I could interact with readers through the blog; not only was it giving me a place to write about my love of food, but it was also enabling me to connect with people all over the world who share my passion. Food brings people together, no matter where in the world they are, or from what walk of life, and the internet, through blogging, social networking sites, and so forth, makes that happen on a scale we could never before have dreamt possible. It's fascinating and liberating and really quite wonderful.

As I continue to grow and develop as a cook I trust my own judgement more and more and I increasingly feel at one with the ingredients I use; really getting to know them, how they like to be handled, how they change when cooked in different ways, which other ingredients they respond to and which they don't. When you start to cook for your own pleasure and your own taste you start to rely on yourself, and the ingredients, as the teacher, and it all becomes much more intuitive. The important thing is not to be afraid of failure, because it's through mistakes and perseverance that we learn, like a toddler learning to walk, stumbling each time but trying again and again, getting that little bit further each time. In cooking you'll learn what works by experiencing what doesn't and the more you try new things the more you'll build your skill and confidence as a cook.

My cooking is heavily influenced by the seasons and the weather. The turning of the season – that cusp when the last hasn't quite departed and the new one hasn't fully arrived – is wonderful to see. I embrace each new season with open arms, welcoming the change it will bring. Cooking can be likened to a sort of pagan magic: the pairing and blending of the ingredients the earth provides, the mixing, the stirring, the tasting, the use of herbs and spices, adding a pinch of this and a pinch of that. When you cook with the seasons you feel at one with nature and in sync' with its natural rhythm. There's a sense of harmony in cooking with fresh herbs and new potatoes in the spring, ripe tomatoes and strawberries in the summer, earthy mushrooms and squashes on autumn days, and robust cabbages and parsnips in the winter.

I love to watch the weather. It affects my mood; the sunshine lifts me, the rain makes me feel nostalgic, the wind unsettles me and the cold weather makes me want to hibernate; and my cooking reflects that. The weather is one of the biggest influences on what I want to eat each day. I like this, it makes me feel balanced and in tune with the elements. Summer is my favourite time of year. I was a summer baby and I adore the sunshine; I love nothing better than a hot, sunny day spent in the great outdoors. But when the long, hot, lazy summer is over I look forward to the contrast of the nights drawing in, and retreating into my warm, cosy home as the cold air descends. This book is filled with recipes and writings for these two extremes and everything in between. These I give to you, from one home cook to another, for this season to the next.

*Julia Parsons, London 2010*

# Cook's notes

Unless otherwise specified eggs are large hen eggs and always free-range. Use eggs at room temperature for the recipes in this book.

For seasoning I use sea salt, which is much less harsh and quite different to processed salt, and freshly ground black pepper.

Parmesan cheese should be Parmigiano Reggiano – the only authentic Parmesan cheese – and always freshly grated.

Wine is like any other ingredient: good quality makes for a good dish. You don't have to pull out an expensive bottle of vintage but you do need to use something that's drinkable. Besides, that way the cook gets a glass too!

Although fruit and vegetables have natural seasons at roughly the same time each year, the changeable weather affects them and so we sometimes see things earlier or later than expected. It's important to remember that nature will tell us when things are ready, not a textbook. So when you go shopping see what home-grown produce is available to buy and work with that. When choosing fruit and vegetables look for those that look fresh and just-picked, with bright colours and no yellowing or browning or wilted leaves.

When buying fish look out for clear indicators of freshness: clear, bright eyes with no cloudiness; vibrant pink or red gills; firm flesh; shiny skin; and a smell of the sea, rather than a strong smell of fish.

Meat should be taken out of the fridge and allowed to come up to room temperature before cooking, to ensure it cooks through properly. This also means that if you're cooking something quickly and rare, such as steak, the middle won't be cold in the middle, making it unpleasant to eat. The cooking times in the recipes in this book are designed for meat at room temperature. If the meat is colder the timings may be out and it may be undercooked.

Many factors affect the cooking times in recipes. All ovens vary and cook at different speeds, depending on whether they are gas, electric or fan assisted, and even then two identical ovens may still have differences in cooking speeds. The recipes in this book, as in all cookbooks, should be taken as a guideline rather than an exact set of instructions never to be wavered from. Get to know your own oven and if you have difficulties with it buy an oven thermometer to check its temperature and go by that.

Finally, use all of your senses when you're cooking: look, listen, touch, smell and taste. And above all, trust your own judgement.

**A note on measurements**

I don't like to be too prescriptive when listing ingredients for recipes – except where it is necessary to be exact – preferring instead to give looser quantities so that you feel you have some creative licence to make the dish as you like it. I'm very much an advocate of adjusting recipes to your own taste and playing around with the ingredients, substituting for what you have in or for what you may prefer. But you may find it useful to understand what I mean when I say 'a knob of butter' or 'a handful of salad leaves'; it's likely that the size of my hands is different to yours, after all! So, here is a quick guide to some of the terms I use throughout this book and their equivalent measures:

all tablespoon and teaspoon measurements are level spoonfuls, not heaped;
a handful of salad leaves is about 30g;
a knob of butter is about 10g;
a bunch of herbs is about 25g;
a handful of cheese is about 35g;
a glass of wine is about 250ml.

# cherry blossom

After the long, cold winter everything comes alive again in the spring, slowly at first, waking leisurely and gently stretching outwards, then bursting into full bloom as the weeks progress. Those first signs of life – the daffodils peeking through the ground, the green leaves forming on the trees, the singing of the new-born birds – bring with them a certain sense of anticipation: change is in the air. As it travels on the breeze it touches the wildlife, the landscape, the life in the ground, and eventually it finds its way through the open window and into the kitchen. My cooking gradually becomes lighter and fresher and I look forward to new seasonal gems becoming the centrepieces of my meals.

For me the promise of the new season starts as early as February, toward the end of winter, with the long awaited purple sprouting broccoli. This beautiful, delicate vegetable is a welcome and exciting arrival after the trusty, but often uninspiring, mid-winter offering. It really brightens up the plate and once it's here I know, no matter how cold and dreary it may still be outside, spring really is on its way.

As spring arrives and starts to take hold other stars of the season present themselves in all their glory: rocket, crisp spring onions, young spinach, tender and sweeter than the more mature leaves, peppery watercress and pea shoots – the delicate yet intensely flavoured leaves of the pea plant. They all hold their own in terms of texture and taste and make for flavoursome and interesting salads. Fresh herbs, such as chives, parsley and mint are plentiful, as is lamb, perfect for the traditional Easter table. Delicious new potatoes begin to arrive now, the cream of the crop being the highly prized Jersey Royals, grown, as the name suggests, exclusively on the island of Jersey. These waxy potatoes with a creamy and mildly nutty taste need nothing more than a knob of butter and a sprinkling of sea salt.

Spring ends on a high note with the prized British asparagus season, short but sweet. Like food lovers all over the country I can't get enough of these glorious spears and I overindulge until the sad day when they disappear, not to be seen again until another year has gone by.

# Spring Vegetable Soup

This lovely light broth, delicately flavoured with sweet vegetables, celebrates the spring harvest. Do feel free to vary the vegetables according to what bounty your garden or allotment produces or what you bring back from the market or shops. Broad beans, courgettes, spring onions or green beans would all be lovely, as would asparagus spears, chopped and added in the last few minutes of simmering.

**Serves 4**

olive oil
2 shallots, finely diced
2 leeks, white and light green parts finely sliced (see Cook's notes)
250g young carrots, peeled or scrubbed and cut into bite-sized pieces
1 litre vegetable stock (see Cook's notes)
100g frozen peas (see Cook's notes)
sea salt and freshly ground black pepper

Heat a little olive oil in a medium pan and add the shallots. Gently sauté them for about 5 minutes, stirring occasionally until they begin to soften then add the leeks and sauté for 1 minute.

Next, add the carrots and vegetable stock to the pan and bring it to the boil. Simmer for about 5 minutes, until the carrots are almost tender, then add the peas and simmer for a further 2 minutes. Season to taste and serve straight away.

**Cook's notes**
Leeks need to be cleaned well as dirt manages to get into them all the way down inside their leaves. The best way to clean them is to slice them in half lengthways, leaving the root on to keep each half together, and then wash them under the tap, fanning out the leaves under the running water. Once you've cleaned them chop off the very dark green parts and save them for the stock pot. Finely slice the white and light green parts for use in the soup.

It's important to use a good stock base for this soup. This base, which the vegetables are suspended in and release their flavour into, is what brings everything together and is the essence of the soup. Home-made stock would be fabulous but in the absence of that use one of the good-quality fresh stocks available from good supermarkets.

Peas are the one vegetable I'm happy to buy frozen as they often taste even better than fresh, with the exception of sweet summer peas fresh from their pods. This is because they are frozen within hours of being picked in order to retain their sweetness, which is lost very quickly when the sugars start turning to starch as soon as they're picked. Choose frozen garden peas or petits pois for the sweetest taste.

# Feta Cheese and Watercress Sauce

Feta cheese is a Greek cheese made with sheep's milk, sometimes combined with a little goat's milk, which is salted and stored in brine. Teaming it with watercress is something that had never occurred to me before I created this recipe but as soon as I did it seemed such an obvious paring; the salty feta and the peppery watercress. The two come together here to create a versatile, creamy sauce that's great for dipping crunchy vegetables into, dressing new potatoes with, or pouring over chicken or steak.

**Makes approximately 450ml**

200g feta cheese
200ml double cream
100g watercress, roughly chopped

Crumble the feta into a medium pan and pour in the double cream. Heat the cream gently, stirring continuously, until the cheese melts completely into it. Continue stirring over a low to medium heat until the mixture thickens.

Stir the watercress into the sauce. Cook it for a few minutes more over a low to medium heat, just to allow the watercress to wilt into it, and then take it off the heat. You shouldn't need to add any seasoning: the feta is salty enough and the watercress mildly peppery.

# Asparagus, Avocado and Pea Shoot Salad

The British asparagus season is far too short, running from late April or early May until the end of June, and knowing this I feast on it as often as I can during that time. There's nothing quite like the taste of fresh British asparagus – jet-lagged, imported stems are simply no match. It's not their fault of course; what hope do they have when, instead of being eaten straight away while they're still bright and sweet, they are forced to travel for hundreds of miles, arriving, finally, on our plates tired from their journey and lifeless? You're much better living without asparagus until the spring and early summer and enjoy it as a seasonal treat. Yes, it is but a short time to enjoy it and a long time until the next season but isn't it all the better, and all the more precious, for the wait?

When it comes to enjoying asparagus, there's nothing nicer than a plate of it simply (and quickly) boiled, steamed or roasted, served with a knob of butter and a sprinkling of sea salt – either as a side dish or on its own in all its splendour. But it's also fabulous in salads such as this one, which with its varying shades of green and fresh flavours, is perfect for spring, either served with grilled chicken or fish or as a starter or main meal in itself.

**Serves 2 as a main course, 4 as a side or starter**

50g pea shoots
2 avocados
12 spears British asparagus, trimmed (see Cook's note)
sea salt

**For the dressing**
1 tablespoon finely chopped fresh mint
2 tablespoons extra virgin olive oil

Arrange the pea shoots on a large serving plate. Cut the avocados in half and remove the stones then, using a spoon, scoop out the flesh in pieces. Scatter the avocado pieces evenly over the pea shoots.

Bring a pan of water, large enough to hold the asparagus, to the boil then add the asparagus spears and cook them for about 3 minutes, until al dente – tender but still a little firm in the middle. Remove the asparagus from the pan as soon as it's cooked. Chop the spears into pieces about 2.5cm long, add them to the salad and season it with a little sea salt.

To make the dressing, mix the mint with the olive oil then drizzle it over the salad just before serving.

**Cook's note**
Unless the asparagus spears are very thin the ends will be woody and will need removing. The best way to do this is to snap the ends off with your hands; asparagus will naturally bend and snap where the woody end begins so you know you're taking it off exactly where you need to. Don't discard the ends; keep them in a bag in the freezer and use them for stock or soup bases, removing and throwing them away when they've given up their flavour to the soup.

# Cheese-smothered New Potatoes

Little new potatoes are so easy to prepare and cook and they taste quite delicious. You can tumble them into one-pot dishes, boil them or roast them without having to do anything to them; they will quite happily cook in their skins and taste great. They're wonderful boiled with a few sprigs of mint and served with nothing more than a knob of butter and a sprinkling of sea salt.

But when I'm feeling naughty I like them this way, under a blanket of melted cheese. They make a great side dish, especially good with lamb or pork chops.

**Serves 4–6**

1kg small new potatoes
200g easy-melting cheese, such as Cheddar, Gruyère or Stilton, grated or crumbled
sea salt

Put the potatoes in a large pan of salted water, bring to the boil and cook for 15–20 minutes or until tender. Drain the potatoes and put them onto a large baking tray in a single layer. Lightly crush the cooked potatoes with a fork and season them with sea salt.

Preheat the grill to high. Sprinkle the grated or crumbled cheese over the potatoes and place them under the hot grill for a few minutes until the cheese melts. Serve immediately.

# Jersey Royal Salad

Jersey Royal potatoes are a real treat and this salad shows them off with simple, complementary ingredients. I like to leave their skins on (and besides, it's easier that way) but you can scrub them off if you prefer.

The use of the shoots of the pea plant as an ingredient in its own right in Britain is a fairly recent one, and a joyous one at that. They're incredibly flavoursome; sweet with a distinct taste of fresh young peas. I love using them in salads and they're quite lovely in this dish with the Jersey Royal Potatoes.

**Serves 4 as a side dish**

500g Jersey Royal potatoes, cut into equal sizes (left whole if very small, or halved)
50g pea shoots
1–2 shallots, finely diced
1–2 tablespoons extra virgin olive oil
sea salt

Put the potatoes in a large pan of salted water, bring to the boil and cook for 15–20 minutes or until tender. Drain and allow the potatoes to cool, until they are just warm; if they are too hot they will wilt the pea shoots.

When the potatoes have cooled put them into a serving bowl and drizzle over the extra virgin olive oil. Add the pea shoots, shallots and a good sprinkling of sea salt. Toss everything together before serving.

**Duck eggs** *are similar in taste to hen eggs but their yolks are so much richer and, for want of a better word, 'eggier'. They have a proportionally larger yolk to white than hen eggs, making them perfect for dipping soldiers into. Not only do they taste wonderful but they keep fresher for longer because their shells are thicker, and they're beautiful to look at too – both the pure white and the pastel blue ones. Use duck eggs in the same way you would hen eggs, but just be aware that they need a little less cooking as they contain less water so quickly turn rubbery. You also need to be careful in baking, because they are larger with different proportions of yolk and white than hen eggs, so they could throw your recipe off. But, with the right recipe they can give fabulous results.*

*Since I discovered the rich taste of duck eggs I've become rather besotted with them and now they're the ones I reach for whenever I want simply cooked eggs, whether boiled, fried, scrambled or made into an omelette. I urge you to try them if you haven't already; they're quite delicious.*

# Duck Egg and Chive Omelette

This makes for a lovely light lunch eaten in the garden on warmer spring days, with a crisp green salad, and a glass of wine in the imitable style of the late English food writer Elizabeth David.

**Serves 1**

3 duck eggs
a small handful of chives, finely
    chopped
a knob of butter
sea salt and freshly ground black
    pepper

Break the eggs into a medium jug and lightly beat them with a fork. Season well, add the chives and gently beat again to combine them with the eggs.

Melt the butter in a large non-stick frying pan, approximately 24cm in diameter, over a medium heat. Once the butter has melted, pour in the beaten eggs then tilt the pan and swirl them around so they coat the bottom leaving no gaps. When the egg just starts to firm up pull one of the edges into the middle using a spatula then tilt the pan to allow the uncooked egg mixture to fill the gap made. Continue this process until the egg is almost, but not completely, set.

At this stage you should take the pan off the heat and fold one side of the omelette into the middle, transfer it to a warmed serving plate and fold the remaining side into the middle so that you have a three fold omelette. Don't worry that the egg isn't completely set as it will continue to cook in the heat it retains once it's left the pan; if you wait for it to set fully in the pan it will quickly over-cook and turn rubbery.

# Softly Scrambled Duck Eggs

I've deliberately called these Softly scrambled duck eggs for an important reason – and one which is not exclusive to duck eggs but applies to hen eggs too. One of the most common mistakes in scrambling eggs is over-cooking them, which leaves them rubbery and unpleasant to eat. They really need only a few minutes of cooking time and they should be creamy and just barely set. So, watch them intently, go easy and think 'softly, softly!'.

**Serves 1**

2 duck eggs
a dash of double cream (optional)
a knob of butter
sea salt and freshly ground black
   pepper

Break the eggs into a medium jug and lightly beat them with a fork. Season well, add the cream, if using, and gently beat again to combine it with the eggs.

Heat the butter over a medium heat in a small non-stick pan and when it starts to gently sizzle pour in the eggs. Stir the eggs continuously with a wooden spoon as they cook,

to scramble them. They will over-cook in seconds so the instant they start to come together – and this will happen quite suddenly after just a minute or so – take the pan off the heat.

Don't worry if the eggs are still a little liquid in places as they will continue to cook in the heat of the pan, just keep stirring them. Remember: you can always put the pan back on the heat if you need to but you can't uncook over-cooked eggs!

# Fried Duck Eggs on Toast

This is one of my favourite weekend breakfasts, to have with a steaming cup of Earl Grey tea. I like my eggs lightly cooked with runny yolks and just-cooked whites, so I fry them over a gentle heat and make sure the pan isn't too hot when they go in.

**Serves 1–2**

olive oil
2 duck eggs
2 slices of bread
butter, for spreading
sea salt

Heat a non-stick medium frying pan over a low to medium heat then add a little olive oil. Carefully crack the eggs open and drop them into the pan without breaking the yolks!

Fry the eggs gently until their whites turn opaque, then spoon over a little of the hot oil onto the yolks to help cook them.

While the eggs are cooking, toast and butter the bread and place on a serving plate. When the eggs are ready, remove them from the pan using a slotted spatula and place them on top of the toast. Finally, sprinkle over a little sea salt before serving.

# Duck Egg Chocolate Cake

This chocolate cake is quite delicious and a great treat for Easter, particularly with the novelty of having been made with duck eggs. The sponge rises beautifully and is not too rich or sweet, which makes for a nice balance with the chocolaty icing.

**For the cake**
50g cocoa powder
175g self-raising flour
225g butter, softened
225g golden caster sugar
4 duck eggs
butter, for greasing

**For the icing**
100g 70% cocoa solids dark
   chocolate
200g butter, softened
200g icing sugar

**To finish**
white or dark chocolate curls or
   grated chocolate (optional)

Grease and line a 20cm round, 7cm deep cake tin using butter and baking parchment. Preheat the oven to 180°C/fan 160°C/gas mark 4.

Sieve the cocoa powder and flour together into a medium mixing bowl so that it's well mixed and then set it aside.

Cream the butter and sugar together in a food mixer until light and fluffy.

Lightly whisk the eggs together and then add the egg mixture little by little, ensuring each drop is incorporated into the butter and sugar mixture before adding more. If the mixture looks like it's starting to curdle add a tablespoon of the flour and cocoa mixture. Finally, gently fold in the remaining flour and cocoa using a metal spoon, being careful not to beat or overwork the mixture, until all the ingredients are completely combined.

Pour the mixture into the prepared cake tin and then bake it for 40–50 minutes, until it feels spongy in the centre. Leave the cake to cool a little in the tin and then turn it out onto a wire rack to cool completely.

To make the icing, melt the chocolate over a bain marie (see Cook's note): fill a small pan about a quarter full with water and bring it to the boil. Break the chocolate into pieces and place it in a small heatproof bowl. Put the bowl over the pan of water, making sure the base doesn't touch the water. Reduce the temperature so the water is just simmering and the steam will gently melt the chocolate. Check occasionally to ensure the pan doesn't boil dry.

Meanwhile, place the butter and sugar in a food mixer and cream them together until very fluffy and almost white. Carefully pour the melted chocolate over the creamed mixture and stir thoroughly to combine. Allow the icing to cool before spreading it over the top and sides of the cake. Decorate the cake with chocolate curls or grated chocolate, if using, before serving it in thick slices.

**Cook's note**
A bain marie, is a container filled with hot water, with a second container suspended over it that holds the ingredients. A bain marie is used when a gentle heat is required as it protects the ingredients from fierce heat and stop them from scorching or cooking too quickly. When chocolate is melted in a bain marie it stops it from seizing and cooking over the heat.

# Steak and Goat's Cheese Salad

My husband Rob cooks a mean steak. Better, I have to begrudgingly concede, than me. If there's a steak in the house to be cooked, Rob's the one to do it; I know when to bow out. He knows the secret to a good steak is a searing hot pan, so hot in fact that he's set the smoke alarm off a few times! To reduce the chance of that happening use as little oil as possible, oil the steak and not the pan, and have a window open to let out the smoke. Rob's preferred tool for the job is a heavy ridged griddle pan, which brands the steaks with charred black marks.

**Serves 4**

olive oil
4 x 200g steaks, cut of your choice but preferably boneless to make slicing easier
2 large handfuls of watercress
2 large handfuls of rocket
200g goat's cheese, with a rind, sliced into 4 rounds
sea salt and freshly ground black pepper

**For the dressing**
2 teaspoons Dijon mustard
2 teaspoons balsamic vinegar
8 tablespoons extra virgin olive oil

Heat a heavy-based, non-stick frying or ridged griddle pan over a high heat until very hot. Brush the steaks on both sides with a little olive oil and season them with salt and black pepper. Cook the steaks in the preheated pan for around 2–4 minutes on each side, depending on their thickness and how you like them cooked (see Cook's note), moving them only to turn them over. When the steaks are cooked, set them aside to rest for 5 minutes, so that their juices can seep back into them, while you prepare the salad.

To make the dressing place all the ingredients into a small bowl and whisk them with a small whisk until they emulsify into a mayonnaise-type consistency. Set the dressing aside.

Arrange the salad leaves onto 4 serving plates. Slice the steaks, I like to slice them fairly thickly, but you may prefer them thinly sliced, and lay them over the salad leaves.

Fry the goat's cheese rounds, in a small frying pan, over a medium heat for 30–60 seconds on each side, just to warm and brown them a little. Arrange the cheese rounds over the steak and salad leaves. Finally, spoon over the dressing just before serving.

**Cook's note**
The best indication of how steaks are cooked is not the clock but how firm they are and how much bounce there is in them when you press on them. The firmer they are and the less bounce they have in them, the more cooked through they are, so rare will be soft and bouncy, well done will be firm, and medium somewhere in between. Once you've cooked a few you'll get to know how they feel when they're done to your liking.

# Baked Camembert with Asparagus Dippers

Surely the very best thing you can do with a whole Camembert, aside from just eating it, is to bake it. The resulting warm, oozing cheese is sublime and cries out for nothing more than something to dip into it like the asparagus spears I suggest here. Make sure you also serve some crusty bread to dip into the cheese that's left once the asparagus has gone, which is likely to happen very quickly indeed!

**Serves 2**

1 x 250g whole Camembert cheese, ideally in a wooden box
12 asparagus spears, trimmed
crusty bread, to serve

Preheat the oven to 220°C/fan 200°C/gas mark 7.

If the Camembert has been packaged in a wooden box take it out and remove all the packaging, then put it back in the box and pop on the lid. Alternatively place the cheese on a large, square, double layer piece of foil and wrap the cheese up to fully enclose it. Make sure there are no gaps for the cheese to escape out of.

Place the cheese, either in its box or wrapped in foil, onto a baking tray (in case of leakage) and then bake it in the oven for 10–15 minutes, until the cheese has melted inside.

To cook the asparagus, bring a large pan of water to the boil then put the spears into the water and simmer them for about 3 minutes or until they are al dente.

Sprinkle a little salt over the asparagus. Dip the warm asparagus and crusty bread into the cheese. Devour!

*Blog entry, April 2008*

I thoroughly enjoyed my solitary walk, looking out from under my colourful umbrella, crunching snow underfoot, passing children making snowmen, a father and daughter having a snowball fight, a fellow photographer. The scenery was wonderful under its blanket of snow. Blossom-filled trees dipping with their heavy loads, flowers in full bloom peeking out from beneath cotton wool snow; how beautiful snow is in the springtime.

# Asparagus, Courgette and Lemon Pasta

Courgettes and asparagus are two of my favourite vegetables; I love their freshness and bite. As strange as this may sound for a vegetable, I think they're actually rather meaty, with a lot of substance to them. They make a great team in this delicious pasta dish, bound together with a lovely lemony sauce. It's fresh and light with great textures and flavours – perfect for a spring lunch shared with friends.

**Serves 4**

**For the pasta**
320g dried pasta shapes, e.g. penne or farfalle
12 asparagus spears, trimmed
a knob of butter
olive oil
1 shallot, finely diced
2 courgettes, halved lengthways and sliced
sea salt and freshly ground black pepper

**For the sauce**
2 egg yolks
juice of 1 lemon
a handful of grated Parmesan cheese
60ml double cream

Bring a large pan of salted water to the boil then add the pasta. Bring the water back up to the boil and cook the pasta according to the pack instructions, until al dente – soft on the outside but still a little firm in the middle.

While the pasta is cooking make the sauce. Place all the sauce ingredients in a jug and using a fork lightly beat them together until they are just combined, then set aside.

Cut each asparagus spear into 4 or 5 pieces and set aside.

Next, melt the butter with a little olive oil in a large frying pan over a medium heat. Add the shallot and sauté it for a minute then add the courgette slices and asparagus pieces. Season with salt and pepper and continue to sauté, turning the vegetables frequently, for 4–5 minutes or until the asparagus and courgettes are cooked, and then remove the pan from the heat.

Drain the cooked pasta, reserving the cooking water. Toss the cooked pasta into the pan containing the vegetables. Add the sauce along with 1–2 tablespoons of the pasta cooking water to loosen it up. It's important to add the sauce to the pan once it has been removed from the heat or the egg yolks will start to cook. Toss everything together to coat in the sauce, season to taste and serve immediately.

# Orange and Rhubarb Jellies

Early rhubarb, available in late winter, is grown inside in dark conditions, making it more colourful, sweeter and more delicate than rhubarb grown outdoors. It's known as forced rhubarb and it's very welcome in the winter when it gives a cheering splash of colour to an otherwise rather muted culinary palette. Its sweet flavour and beautiful pink colour is ideal for jellies such as these. You can use outdoor grown rhubarb but you won't get quite the same pretty pink colour.

**Makes 4–6 jellies**

1kg rhubarb, preferably forced, cut into pieces approximately 2cm long
300g caster sugar
juice of 1 orange
100ml Cointreau
7 leaves of platinum grade gelatine

Put the rhubarb into a large pan along with the sugar and orange juice then simmer it over a gentle heat for about 20 minutes, until it's soft and has released its juices.

Take the rhubarb mixture off the heat. Place a sieve over a medium bowl and strain the rhubarb through the sieve, pressing it through with the back of a metal spoon. Stir the Cointreau into the rhubarb liquid.

Soak the gelatine leaves in water, according to the packet instructions, then add them to the rhubarb liquid, stirring to dissolve them.

Allow the rhubarb liquid to cool before pouring it into small individual moulds or glasses. Put them into the fridge overnight or through the day to allow jellies to set.

Once they're set turn the jellies out of their moulds or serve them in the glasses. To make turning them out easier, dip the moulds briefly in hot water to loosen the jellies away from the sides.

**Cook's note**
Stir the rhubarb left into the sieve into some Greek yogurt or double cream for a quick pudding.

# Rhubarb Crumble

In the spring outdoor rhubarb becomes available, which is perfect for rhubarb crumble; surely one of the cheeriest of all home-made puddings. Sinking your spoon into a crumbly, golden, biscuit-like topping and through to hot, sweet and tart pink fruit beneath is incredibly joyful, especially if there's thick, hot custard too. It certainly puts a smile on my face!

**Serves 4**

**For the fruit**
800g rhubarb, cut into pieces
    approximately 2cm long
100g caster sugar, plus extra to
    taste

**For the topping**
240g plain flour
140g cold butter, cut into small
    cubes
80g caster sugar

double cream or Home-made
    Custard (see page 166), to serve
    (optional)

Preheat the oven to 200°C/fan 180°C/gas mark 6.

Put the rhubarb and 100g of sugar into a medium pan along with 3 tablespoons of water and cook it over a low to medium heat, stirring regularly so that it cooks evenly, for about 10 minutes, until the pieces are starting to soften but are still whole. Check for sweetness and add more sugar if required.

To make the topping place the flour, butter and sugar in a medium mixing bowl and rub it together with your fingertips until you get a breadcrumb-like mixture. You can use a food processor but you need to be careful not to over-process it. I personally prefer to use my fingers to keep it light and to be able to tell exactly when the texture is just how I like it.

Put the rhubarb into 22cm round or square, 8cm deep ovenproof dish and loosely sprinkle the crumble mixture over the fruit, covering it completely. Don't pat the topping down and compress it or it will become heavy and stodgy. Bake the crumble for 30–40 minutes, until the topping is golden and the rhubarb tender and bubbling up underneath.

Serve the crumble just as it is or with double cream or Home-made Custard if you prefer.

# Cinnamon Hearts

These sugar sweet biscuits are so much fun to make. Not only do they make the house smell heart-warmingly of cinnamon as they bake but they allow you to have fun with playdough-like fondant icing and cookie cutters. And when you've had your fun you can make someone's day by popping them into a little box lined with baking parchment or wrapping them in pretty cellophane and giving them as a gift.

**Makes approximately 12 large biscuits**

100g unsalted butter, softened
100g caster sugar
1 large egg, beaten
250g plain flour, plus extra for
    dusting
1 teaspoon ground cinnamon
400g fondant icing
food colouring (see Cook's notes)

Line 2 baking trays with baking parchment.

Cream the butter and sugar together in a food mixer until light and fluffy. Gradually add the beaten egg to the butter and sugar, mixing it in as you add it. Finally sieve in the flour and cinnamon, and bring everything together with your hands to form a dough. Wrap the dough in foil or clingfilm then chill it in the fridge for at least half an hour before using it.

Once the dough has chilled, preheat the oven to 180°C/fan 160°C/gas mark 4.

The chilled dough will still be fairly sticky so you'll need to roll it out on a well-floured surface and sprinkle over more flour as needed. Roll it out until it's about 3mm thick. Cut out heart shapes using a heart shaped biscuit cutter, approximately 10cm in diameter (although you could of course use any cutter if you don't have a heart shaped one) and place them on the lined baking trays.

Bake the biscuits for about 10 minutes, but do keep an eye on them; they may need a few minutes less or longer. They should be very lightly golden when cooked. When they're ready put them onto a wire rack to cool.

To colour the fondant icing, place it in a large bowl and add a small amount of food colouring; start with just a tiny amount as it's very intense and you can always add

more if necessary. To distribute the colour kneed the icing with the palm of your hand, continually bringing the icing from the outside edge into its middle until the colour is even throughout.

Once you've coloured the icing, dust the icing with flour and roll it out a little thinner than the biscuits. Cut out heart shapes using the same cutter you used for the biscuits. Brush the underside of the hearts with water, using a pastry brush, and place them over the biscuits, gently rubbing over the icing to help it stick.

**Cook's notes**
I use gel food colouring as it's so much nicer than liquid ones and has a greater colour intensity. A wider choice of colours are available too.

I like to decorate the biscuits with fondant flowers, cut out using a very small flower cutter, from fondant in a contrasting colour to the biscuits, stuck on using a little water. If you want to try this, reserve some of the fondant and colour it a different colour.

# sunshine and lemons

When I look back at my childhood many of my happiest memories are of the summertime: playing outside all afternoon and into the early evening; blackberry picking with my mum and my sister; lying on freshly cut grass making daisy chains. Perhaps that's why it's my favourite time of year and why I love nothing more than being outside in the warm air soaking up the sunshine on long, lazy afternoons that stop time.

It's the simple things that come to my mind when I think of summer: the smell of freshly cut grass; windows flung wide open; butterflies dancing on a light breeze; warm sunshine on bare skin; washing gently blowing on the line; the buzz of a passing bee; the sound of playing children shrieking with laughter. Life seems so free and easy, I feel younger, more alive, more carefree, and my cooking reflects that with vibrant colours, sharp and zesty flavours that explode on your tongue, fresh, crunchy vegetables and fruity puddings.

The hot weather cries out for easy, laid back food. Simple, fresh ingredients requiring minimum effort and cooking; less structure, more flow. And the beauty of it is that summer produce lends itself so easily to that. At this time of year fruit and vegetables are bursting with flavour and are so good you can let them speak for themselves; they need very little doing to them – the simpler, the better. On the hottest of days you want light, refreshing food such as crisp salads, zingy sorbets and fruity drinks, and when the weather is more like autumn than summer – which is often the case here in Britain – we need a reminder of the sunshine with bright plates of colourful summer food.

# Home-made Lemonade

When the sun is beating down, there's nothing quite as welcoming or refreshing as a jug of ice-cold, home-made lemonade. It's as easy as making a cup of tea and a dream to drink on a hot summer's day.

**Makes approximately 1 litre**

4 large unwaxed lemons
  (see Cook's notes)
200ml boiling water
approximately 80g caster sugar,
  to taste
approximately 600ml chilled still
  or sparkling water, to dilute
ice and lemon slices, to serve

Peel the skin off the lemons in large strips using a potato peeler, leaving the bitter white pith on them. Half the lemons and squeeze them to remove all the juice. Add the strips of lemon peel and juice to the boiling water. Add 80g of caster sugar and stir well until it dissolves. Set aside to cool. Once the liquid has cooled you can either use it straight away or chill it in the fridge. If you like a strong lemon flavour leave the lemon peel in, until you are ready to drink the lemonade.

To serve, pass the mixture through a sieve then dilute it with 600ml of the still or sparkling water. Check the taste and add more sugar or water if necessary. Serve in a big jug with lots of ice and slices of lemon.

**Cook's notes**
Lemons are sometimes lightly coated with wax to prolong their lifespan but you don't really want wax in your lemonade, so it's best to choose unwaxed lemons.

Rather than chopping up the whole lemons for the lemonade, I peel and then juice them, leaving the white pith behind as this is quite bitter.

I like my lemonade quite strong and lemony, but you can adjust the amount of sugar and water to balance the lemon flavour according to your own taste.

To make pink lemonade stir 3 or 4 crushed raspberries into the mixture just before you sieve it, or for a grown-up-only version try diluting the lemon mixture with sparkling medium dry or sweet white wine instead of water.

# Lemon, Chicken and Spring Onion Salad

I love the zing and sharpness of the lemon in this salad, softened and made palatable by a little sugar in the dressing. It works so well with the chicken and crisp spring onions, making this one of my favourite summer salads.

**Serves 2 as a main course or 4 as a starter**

4 large handfuls of salad leaves, e.g. rocket, watercress and spinach
150g cooked chicken, chopped or shredded into large pieces (leftover roast chicken is perfect)
2 spring onions, finely sliced

**For the dressing**
2 lemons
1–2 teaspoons caster sugar
2 tablespoons extra virgin olive oil

Lay the salad leaves on a plate and scatter over the chicken and spring onions.

To make the dressing, chop the ends off the lemons then stand each one on end and carefully slice the skin and pith off the sides. Cut the flesh into tiny pieces, as small as you can, discarding the pips along the way, then put them into a bowl along with all the juice on the chopping board, sugar to taste and the olive oil. Mix everything well, ensuring the sugar dissolves, then spoon the dressing over the salad.

# Chicken and Avocado Salad

I'm disappointed if there are no leftovers when I roast a chicken; I love them so. Thankfully this doesn't happen very often as I usually cook a chicken for just Rob and me so there's plenty left. Even when we do our worst and all the breast meat is gone there's still a surprising amount of meat not only on the legs but also underneath the chicken, where it's succulent and full of flavour.

A roast chicken sandwich made with thick crusty bread and mayonnaise is hard to beat but there are plenty of other options for leftover chicken: pasta bakes, soups, stir fries, pies, risotto. In the summer I love it in simple salads like this classic chicken avocado.

**Serves 2 as a main course or 4 as a starter**

3 handfuls of salad leaves, e.g. romaine, lollo rosso and frisée
150g cooked chicken, chopped or shredded into large pieces
2 ripe avocados, halved and stoned
$\frac{1}{2}$ lemon
extra virgin olive oil
sea salt

Lay the salad leaves on a plate and scatter over the chicken. Cut each avocado half into three slices. Using a sharp knife, remove the skin from each avocado slice. Arrange the avocado slices over the leaves and chicken. Drizzle a squeeze of lemon juice and some extra virgin olive oil over the salad and finally season with sea salt.

# Roast Beef Salad

The salad is fabulous presented on a huge platter to family and friends, and is ideal for using up leftover roast beef or as a summer alternative to the roast dinner – in fact it's worth roasting a joint of beef just for this purpose. It's big on flavour with the beef, red onion, tomatoes and fiery red chilli brought together with the tangy balsamic dressing. Use good quality tomatoes, preferably on the vine, and as much or as little chilli as you like.

**Serves 4–6**

**For the salad**
150g mixed salad leaves such as spinach, red chard, watercress or rocket
1 red onion, halved and finely sliced
4 large tomatoes, finely sliced
12 slices rare roast beef
1–2 red chillies, deseeded and finely chopped
sea salt

**For the dressing**
1 tablespoon balsamic vinegar
3 tablespoons extra virgin olive oil

Lay the salad leaves over a large platter. Arrange the red onion and tomato slices over the leaves. Sprinkle the tomatoes with sea salt. Lay the slices of roast beef over the salad and sprinkle over the chilli.

Place the balsamic vinegar and olive oil in a small jug, whisk it together with a fork then drizzle it over the salad before serving.

# Green Bean and Herb Rice

This vibrant and fragrant rice dish makes a great accompaniment to fish or meat and is just as nice served hot or cold. The white basmati rice is beautifully flecked with subtly different shades of green and all the textures and flavours mingle together.

In the spring and summer I grow my own herbs in pots and it's wonderful to be able to step out of my kitchen and into the garden and cut big handfuls of fresh green herbs to chop and throw into the rice. They're as easy as anything to grow and it's so convenient to have them all there rather than having to buy small packets of herbs from the supermarket – not to mention much cheaper. I love inhaling their heady fragrance as I walk past; it's like aromatherapy in my own garden.

**Serves 6**

300g basmati rice, rinsed under cold running water
200g green beans, trimmed
30g mixed soft herbs (eg. basil, flat leaf parsley, chives and mint), finely chopped
4 spring onions, finely chopped (optional)
sea salt and freshly ground black pepper

Bring a large pan of water to the boil and then add the rice. Cook for 8-10 minutes until the rice is cooked through and then drain it.

While the rice is cooking, bring a medium pan of water to the boil. Add the beans to the boiling water and cook them for 5 minutes. Drain and cut them each into 4 small pieces.

Add the herbs and spring onions, if using, to the rice along with the beans, mixing everything together, then season well.

**Cook's note**
If you decide to serve this dish cold it's important to cool the rice quickly. Once it is cool, cover and store it in the fridge immediately and eat within one day.

# Red Apple and Parma Ham Salad

The vibrant red and white of the apples against the green back drop of the watercress, rocket and spinach make this a beautiful salad. It has lots of interest too: the combination of Parma ham, apple and white balsamic vinegar make it deliciously sweet, juicy and salty, and the crisp apple and salad leaves give it good texture.

**Serves 2 as a main course or 4 as a starter**

**for the salad**

4 handfuls of mixed watercress, rocket and spinach leaves
1 red apple, cored and sliced into sixteenths
6 slices Parma ham, torn into strips

**for the dressing**

1 tablespoon white balsamic vinegar
3 tablespoons extra virgin olive oil

ciabatta bread, to serve

Lay the salad leaves onto individual plates or one large serving dish. Arrange the apple slices and ham over the leaves. Finally, combine the oil and vinegar in a small jug, whisk well with a fork and drizzle it over the salad. Serve with warm ciabatta bread.

As I sat on the train this morning, open book in hand, vaguely looking out of th

# Chorizo and New Potato Salad

This tasty salad is perfect for a hot
summer's day, bringing a little of
the Mediterranean to England.
The trilogy of chorizo, peppers,
and tomatoes is quite spectacular
and the potatoes soak up all that
wonderful flavour.

**Serves 2 as a main course or
4 as a starter**

400g new potatoes, cut into equal
    sizes (left whole if very small,
    or halved)
120g uncooked chorizo, skinned
    and diced
1 red pepper, cut into small dice
150g cherry tomatoes, halved
a handful of rocket
sea salt
crusty bread, to serve

Put the potatoes in a large pan of
salted water, bring to the boil and
cook for 15–20 minutes or until
tender. Drain and set aside.

Fry the chorizo in a large frying pan
over a medium heat for 3–4 minutes
until it releases its oil. Then turn
up the heat a little and add the
pepper and potatoes and cook for
6–8 minutes. Add the tomatoes and
cook for a further couple of
minutes, until the potatoes have
turned golden and the chorizo is
cooked through.

Put the potato and chorizo mixture
onto plates then top with the rocket
and sprinkle over some sea salt to
season. Serve with crusty bread.

# Pea-stuffed Chicken Breasts with Parmesan Crusts

The appearance of fresh peas in their pods is one of the highlights of the culinary calendar for me. They're so incredibly sweet you can eat them straight from their pod; delicious to snack on or to have in salads. If I am cooking them I have to buy more than I need as I can't resist popping them into my mouth as I shell them! I have vivid memories of sitting up at the kitchen table as a child, shelling peas with my sister, a big bowl between us, doing exactly the same thing.

For this dish the peas are puréed and stuffed into a chicken breast which is then coated in Parmesan breadcrumbs and baked. It's lovely to make in the height of summer, served with a crisp green salad.

**Serves 4**

500g fresh peas in their pods (approximately 150g shelled weight)
100g fresh or dried white breadcrumbs
2 handfuls finely grated Parmesan cheese
1 large egg, beaten
4 boned and skinned chicken breasts
sea salt and freshly ground black pepper

Preheat the oven to 190°C/fan 170°C/gas mark 5.

Bring a small pan of water to the boil while you shell the peas. Add them to the water once it's boiling then simmer them until tender, which will take approximately 5 minutes. Once they're cooked, drain them (reserve the cooking water) and blend them to a thick purée using a hand-held blender, adding a little of the reserved cooking water if necessary.

Mix the breadcrumbs and Parmesan in a large bowl, season and set aside. Put the beaten egg into a separate bowl, large enough to hold one of the chicken breasts.

Using a sharp knife, slit each chicken breast lengthways to form a pocket. Fill each pocket with one quarter of the pea purée. Secure the edges of each chicken breast with a couple of cocktail sticks to ensure the filling stays in. Carefully put one of the chicken breasts into the bowl containing the beaten egg and spoon the egg over to coat. Transfer the chicken into the Parmesan breadcrumbs and coat it completely with the breadcrumbs. Place the chicken on a non-stick baking tray. Repeat for the remaining chicken breasts.

Bake the chicken for 30–35 minutes, or until the breadcrumbs are golden and the chicken is cooked through (carefully pierce it through the middle and make sure the juices run clear).

**Cook's note**
Keep the pea pods for use in stock or to flavour soups (removing them at the end). They keep very well in the freezer.

# Apple and Raspberry Tart

This sweet, summery tart is
delicious warm with a dollop of
cream but is just as nice eaten cold
as a snack.

375g ready-rolled puff pastry
2 sweet eating apples, such as
    Royal Gala or Pink Lady, cored
    and thinly sliced
a little melted butter, for brushing
1 egg, beaten, for glazing (optional)
120g raspberries
2 tablespoons caster sugar

Preheat the oven to 200°C/
fan 180°C/gas mark 6. Line a large
baking tray with baking parchment.

Place the pastry on the lined
baking tray. Using a sharp knife,
score lines around all four sides of
the pastry, about 3cm from the
edge, being careful not to cut all
the way through. This will allow
the edges to puff up nicely.

Lay the apple slices over the pastry
in three neat lines, overlapping a
little if necessary, keeping within
the scored edges. Brush the apples
with the melted butter. For an
optional glossy finish brush the
pastry with the beaten egg.

Bake the tart in the middle of the
oven for 10 minutes. Scatter the
raspberries over the apple slices
and sprinkle over the caster sugar.
Cook the tart for a further 10
minutes or until the pastry is puffed
up and golden.

# Peaches and Cream Trifle

This is such a lovely trifle, made even peachier through roasting the peaches to bring out their flavour. When making it, whip the cream very lightly so that it gently flops over the custard, peaches and schnapps-soaked sponge.

**Serves 6**

4 ripe peaches, quartered and stoned
25g butter
25g caster sugar
240g Madeira cake
50–100ml peach schnapps
500ml Home-made (see page 166) or
    ready-made fresh chilled custard

300ml double cream, lightly whipped
chopped or sliced nuts, such as
    pistachios or almonds, to decorate

Preheat the oven to 200°C/
fan 180°C/gas mark 6.

Put the peach quarters into an ovenproof dish, dot the butter over them and sprinkle over the sugar. Bake them for 15 minutes then allow them to cool.

Meanwhile, slice the Madeira cake and line the bottom of a glass trifle bowl with it. Drizzle over a little peach schnapps and set aside for the sponge to soak it up.

Repeat until all the schnapps is used up or the sponge won't absorb any more.

When the peach quarters have cooled lay them on top of the Madeira cake and drizzle over a little of the peach cooking juices. Cover the peaches with the custard, smoothing it out with the back of a metal spoon. Spoon the whipped cream on top and spread it out in an even layer to cover the custard and sprinkle with the nuts to serve.

# Tipsy Raspberries and Cream

Fresh, ripe raspberries in season are so beautiful and full of flavour that they need very little doing to them. This simple dessert uses raspberry liqueur to bring out the best in them and then dresses them up with whipped cream.

**Serves 4**

400g raspberries
4 tablespoons raspberry liqueur
1 tablespoon icing sugar
200ml double cream, lightly
    whipped

Place the raspberries in a medium bowl, pour over the liqueur and add the icing sugar, then stir the ingredients together, very gently so as not to break the raspberries, until well combined.

Put the raspberries into 4 individual glasses or bowls and top each with a dollop of the cream.

# Summer Pavlova

The illustrious Pavlova dessert was dreamt up in honour of the famous ballerina Anna Pavlova. You can certainly see the likeness to a ballerina's tutu in the billowing mounds of whipped egg whites and sugar. It makes for a spectacular dessert that never fails to impress and yet is as simple as anything to make.

**Serves 8–10**

**For the base**
4 egg whites
220g caster sugar
1 teaspoon white wine vinegar

**For the topping**
400ml double cream, lightly
    whipped
400g prepared mixed soft fruit such
    as strawberries raspberries,
    blueberries and cherries
icing sugar, for dusting (optional)

Preheat the oven to 140°C/ fan 120°C/gas mark 1.

Place the egg whites into a food mixer. Whisk the eggs until they form stiff peaks (see Cook's notes). Next gradually add the caster sugar, one tablespoon at a time, whisking each tablespoon in before adding the next. Once all the sugar has been incorporated and dissolved the mixture should be firm and glossy, and not feel gritty – test this by taking a pinch of the mixture and rubbing it between your finger and thumb. Finally whisk in the white wine vinegar.

Dot a little of the mixture into each corner of a sheet of baking parchment then turn it over and stick it onto a large baking tray. You may find it helpful to first draw a circle on the parchment, approximately 24cm in diameter, to guide you when shaping the meringue. If you do, makes sure you turn the paper over so that the pencil markings are face down on the tray.

Pour the mixture onto the baking parchment and spread it out with a spatula to make a circular shape about 24cm in diameter, flattened in the middle and raised a little around the edges.

Bake the meringue in the oven for 1 hour, then turn the oven off and leave the meringue inside to dry out for several hours, until the oven is completely cool – ideally overnight.

Just before you are ready to serve the Pavlova, spread the whipped cream over the meringue and arrange the fruits on top. For extra decoration dust a little icing sugar over the fruits, if desired, before serving.

**Cook's notes**
The classic Pavlova recipe uses white wine vinegar and cornflour, for a chewy marshmallow-like centre but I prefer to just use the vinegar so that the Pavlova is fluffy in the middle without the chewiness.

The egg whites are whisked sufficiently when you can hold the bowl upside down without them falling out. This can be quite worrying the first few times you do it but they really won't fall out if they're whisked enough, I promise!

# Cherry Pie

To be perfectly honest, I'm not sure that any cherry pie can live up to the one in my head: the one with crumbly pastry and glossy, jammy cherries bursting with deep flavour; the one that tells stories of summertime and of family life around the kitchen table; the one that offers nourishment and love with every bite. So here I offer you just a humble pie, but one that makes me very happy. Eat a slice of it warm with cold vanilla ice cream and tell me the world isn't a better place.

**Serves 6**

**For the shortcrust pastry**
150g cold butter, cut into small cubes
300g plain flour, sieved
butter, for greasing
flour, for dusting

**For the filling**
600g cherries, pitted (see Cook's notes)
a squeeze of lemon juice (optional)
2–4 tablespoons caster sugar, depending on the sweetness of the cherries
2 tablespoons cornflour
2 tablespoons Kirsch
1 egg, beaten
vanilla ice cream, to serve

Grease a 23cm round pie tin with butter.

Start by making the pastry. Rub the butter into the flour in a medium mixing bowl using your fingertips until it resembles breadcrumbs. Add 2 tablespoons of cold water to the mixture and stir it with a round bladed knife to bring it together. Slowly add a little more water if necessary, and then use your hands to form a smooth ball of dough. Wrap the pastry in foil or clingfilm and chill it in the fridge for 30 minutes.

Place the pitted cherries in a bowl. Taste one of the cherries and if they are quite sweet you may like to add a squeeze of lemon juice to cut through their sweetness. Sprinkle the cherries with the sugar, cornflour and liqueur and mix everything together well, coating the cherries thoroughly. Set them aside for at least 30 minutes.

When you're ready to put the pie together, preheat the oven to 190°C/fan 170°C/gas mark 5.

Divide the pastry into two equal halves. Dust the worksurface with flour and roll out one half of the pastry into a circle large enough to line the pie tin. Lay it in the bottom of the tin and press it down around the edges of the tin, then fill it with the cherry mixture. Roll out the second piece of pastry and top the pie with it, pressing it down well around the edges to seal it. Make a small hole in the middle of the pastry

to let the steam escape when the pie is cooking. Brush the pastry with the beaten egg and bake the pie for 40–45 minutes or until lightly golden.

**Cook's notes**
The only sensible way to consider pitting the cherries is with a cherry pitter; it makes the job so much easier. But make sure you wear an apron to protect you from the spray of juice and have a cloth handy to wipe down the sides because the juice goes everywhere!

If you prefer you can make the pastry in a food processor.

Blog entry,
September 2008

'...the nights are drawing in and the mornings are chillier; summer has its back turned and is on its way home.'

# Last Summer Fling Crumble

I first made this crumble as a final farewell to the summer of 2008, with the last strawberries of the year. As though defying the onset of autumn I threw in a punnet each of raspberries and blueberries and, in what can only described as an act of unadulterated extravagance, a whole bar of white chocolate. It was wickedly good.

**Serves 4**

**For the fruit**
300g strawberries, hulled (see Cook's notes)
200g blueberries
200g raspberries
50–100g white chocolate, broken into small pieces (see Cook's notes)

**For the topping**
240g plain flour
140g cold butter, cut into small cubes
80g caster sugar

Preheat the oven to 200°C/ fan 180°C/Gas Mark 6.

Place the fruit in a 22cm round or square, 8cm deep ovenproof dish and then evenly scatter over the pieces of chocolate.

Put the flour, butter and sugar in a medium mixing bowl and rub it together with your fingertips until you get a breadcrumb-like mixture. Loosely pile the crumble over the fruit and chocolate. Bake the crumble for 35–40 minutes, until the topping is golden and the mixture bubbling up underneath.

**Cook's notes**
To hull strawberries means to remove the green leaves, white tops and core from them. Carefully use a small paring knife to do this.

The chocolate makes the fruit very sweet, so if you prefer it a little sharper use only 50g.

# poppy fields

I love to eat al fresco, whether lazily snacking at a picnic, enjoying burgers with friends at a barbecue or simply eating hot, salty chips straight from the wrapper as I walk home. The great outdoors seems to bring on a hunger like no other, senses are heightened and everything smells and tastes so much better. It doesn't even matter if it's cold outside when you have hot food to warm you from the inside out. I'll never forget the time back in my teens when I was out with a group of friends and we stopped to pick up another friend on our way. Her mother gave her a piping hot baked potato, the bottom half wrapped snugly in tin foil, the top opened up and the insides sprinkled with salt and mashed with butter until fluffy. She ate it with a fork as we walked along in the cold night air. How I longed for that potato!

But of course the very best time to eat outside is in the summertime, when the sun is shining and the skies are clear and blue. When the weather is warm it's nice to serve lunch for friends in the garden to make a change from the dining room. For a sense of occasion dress up your garden table with a crisp cotton tablecloth and fresh flowers and serve Prosecco, my favourite al fresco wine; it tastes like someone shook up summer, making it fizzy and frothy, and bottled it!

I long to be outside in the fresh air in the summertime and I love nothing more on a sunny afternoon than taking a picnic hamper to a grassy park or a field and laying down a rug. And when the sun and the food have made me sleepy I like to lie back and rest. Idly running your fingertips over the grass whilst looking up at a blue, cloudless sky is wonderfully therapeutic. In that time nothing matters; cares simply evaporate into the summer breeze. Those moments are worth so much; they enliven and refresh the soul and leave you feeling at one with nature and the world.

# Chilled Cherry Tomato and Basil Soup

The intoxicating flavours of the sweet cherry tomatoes and the herby basil in this soup give you an intense hit of summer. The tomatoes are roasted to deepen their flavour and the basil is added right at the end to keep it fresh tasting in the soup.

It's unusual for me to make a chilled soup as I generally dislike them. I tend to equate soup with warmth and comfort on blustery days and so a chilled one seems to be all wrong. But when I first made this soup and put my associations to one side, considering only the vivid flavours of the cherry tomatoes and the basil, I discovered how wonderfully refreshing it is as a summer cooler; incredibly good to eat outside in the garden on a scorching day.

**Serves 4**

1kg cherry tomatoes, preferably on
   the vine
olive oil
$\frac{1}{2}$ celery stick, finely chopped
1 shallot, finely chopped
500ml vegetable stock
25g fresh basil, stalks removed
sea salt and freshly ground black
   pepper

Preheat the oven to 200°C/
fan 180°C/gas mark 6.

Remove the tomatoes from their vines and put them into a roasting tray. Drizzle them with olive oil and then roast them for 20 minutes.

Meanwhile in a large pan heat a little olive oil and sauté the celery and shallot over a medium heat for a couple minutes until softened. Add the roasted tomatoes and stock to the pan then remove the pan from the heat. Blend the mixture in the pan with a hand blender, to a make a smooth purée.

Pass the soup through a fine sieve to remove any remaining pieces of vegetables and the tomato skins. Stir the basil leaves into the sieved mixture and blend the soup one final time. Season according to taste.

Chill the soup well in the fridge before serving so that it's cooling and refreshing.

**Cook's note**
Although this is first and foremost a chilled soup, I gave this recipe to my friend Nicole and she tells me she regularly enjoys it as a hot soup, so do feel free to serve it hot or cold, as you wish.

# Cherry Tomato and Mint Salsa

I adore small, sweet, cherry tomatoes, bursting with flavour; they bring sunshine right onto my plate whatever the weather. They're fabulous in salads and are also nice pan-fried or roasted on the vine, which deepens their flavour, and served as an accompaniment to fish or meat.

This salsa really celebrates the flavour of the tomatoes. The sea salt brings out that flavour and the fresh mint enlivens it, waking up your taste buds. I've become somewhat addicted to it, eating it throughout the summer. Use the best quality tomatoes you can find and buy them on the vine for the sweetest, most intense taste.

**Serves 4**

400g cherry tomatoes, preferably
   on the vine
1 teaspoon sea salt
2 tablespoons finely chopped mint
   leaves
1 tablespoon extra virgin olive oil

Chop the tomatoes into quarters, or eighths if they're quite large and place them in a small bowl. Add the salt and mix well. Leave the tomatoes to stand for 10 minutes and then drain off the juice that seeps out of them.

Add the mint and the olive oil to the chopped tomatoes and stir well. Drain off any excess juice once more before serving. This is nice served either chilled or at room temperature but is best eaten within an hour or so of making.

**Cook's notes**
This salsa is incredibly versatile and is particularly good with griddled meats such as lamb chops. I often serve it at barbecues.

# Summer Salad

This salad is big and bold with a classic combination of Mediterranean favourites. When you have ripe, good quality ingredients you need add nothing but a sprinkling of sea salt.

**Serves 2 as a main course, 4 as a starter**

4 ripe tomatoes, sliced
2 ripe avocados. halved and stoned
2 x 125g balls buffalo mozzarella cheese
6 slices Parma ham
sea salt
focaccia or ciabatta, to serve

Arrange the tomato slices on individual plates or a large serving dish. Cut each avocado half into three slices. Using a sharp knife, remove the skin from each avocado slice and lay them over the tomatoes.

Tear or slice the mozzarella into medium-sized pieces and lay them over the tomato and avocado slices. Tear the Parma ham into large strips and lay them over the cheese. Finally sprinkle over some sea salt. Serve with bread.

# Eton Mess

This very English summer dessert originates from Eton College, where it's traditionally served in June at the annual prize-giving ceremony. I sometimes like to add pieces of white chocolate to the fabulously gooey mixture for an extra special, albeit untraditional, treat.

**Serves 4–6**

8 meringue nests
450g strawberries, hulled and roughly chopped
300g double cream, lightly whipped
100g white chocolate, roughly chopped (optional)

Break up the meringue nests and put them into a large mixing bowl along with the strawberries, whipped cream and chocolate, if using. Roughly mix everything together then transfer it to serving dishes.

**Cook's notes**
You can either buy the meringue nests or make your own following the Strawberry Chocolate Meringues recipe on page 112.

# Watermelon, Blueberry and Mint Salad

This is a sweet yet refreshing salad, quite lovely when the sun is shining. The juice of an orange adds a subtle flavour – you probably wouldn't even taste it if you didn't know it was there – but it helps to bring out the flavour of the watermelon and blueberries and gives them a delicately sweet, glossy coating.

**Serves 4–6**

$1/2$ watermelon, chopped into
    bite-sized pieces
200g blueberries
juice of 1 orange
2 tablespoons caster sugar
1 handful fresh mint leaves,
    chopped

Combine the watermelon and blueberries in a large serving bowl.

In a small pan heat the orange juice and sugar together, bring it up to a boil and then gently simmer it, stirring occasionally, until it reduces by half and is a little syrupy. Allow it to cool and then pour it over the fruits, tossing them to cover them all in it.

You can serve the salad straight away but it's even better if left for 30 minutes or so to let the flavours further develop.

Sprinkle the mint over just before serving.

# Midsummer Cake

I used to love watching, and helping, my mum make cakes when I was a child and I love making them myself just as much now. What a sense of achievement, to bake your very own cake from just a few basic ingredients!

This is a classic Victoria Sponge cake except that it contains lemon zest and is filled with thick double cream and summer fruits instead of the traditional raspberry jam. It's the perfect cake for a very English afternoon tea. Its name came from the children's novel *I Capture the Castle* and although the cake isn't described in the book the name caught my attention and immediately had me thinking about what such a cake may be like. This is how I like to imagine it.

**Serves 6–8**

**For the cake**
175g butter, softened
175g caster sugar
zest of 1 lemon (optional)
3 eggs
175g self-raising flour, sifted
butter, for greasing

**For the filling**
150ml double cream, whipped
50g strawberries, hulled
50g blueberries
50g raspberries

**To decorate**
icing sugar, for dusting
a few berries (optional)

Preheat the oven to 180°C/fan 160°C/gas mark 4.

Grease and line 2 x 18cm round cake tins.

Cream the butter and sugar together in a food mixer until light and fluffy. Stir in the lemon zest, if using.

Lightly whisk the eggs together and then add the egg mixture little by little, ensuring each drop is incorporated into the butter and sugar mixture before adding more. If the mixture looks like it's starting to curdle add a tablespoon of the flour. Finally, gently fold in the remaining flour using a metal spoon, being careful not to beat or overwork the mixture, until all the ingredients are completely combined.

Divide the mixture between the lined tins and smooth the tops with a palette knife.

Bake the cakes for 20–25 minutes, until they're light golden and springy to the touch. Allow the cakes to cool a little in the tins and then turn them out on a wire rack to cool completely.

Once the cakes are cool spoon the whipped cream onto one of them and spread it out into an even layer. Arrange the berries evenly over the cream and place the second cake on top. Dust over some icing sugar, and place a few berries on top if you like, for decoration and serve straight away.

# Iced Orange Wedges

I like to have a bag of frozen orange wedges in my freezer in the summer. They make for a refreshing iced snack in the middle of the afternoon when the sun is beating down and they make great ice cubes too, in a glass of orange juice, lemonade or a vodka and orange. Simply cut oranges into eights (keeping the peel on) and pop them into a bag and into the freezer. If the wedges stick together once they are frozen, give the bag a bang on the kitchen counter to free them.

# Pimm's and Lemonade

Pimm's is surely the quintessential English summer drink. Wonderfully refreshing with a hint of spiciness, it's absolutely delicious laced with fruit and mint and is always a hit at a barbecue or garden party.

For the perfect Pimm's and lemonade fill a glass with ice and pour in 1 part Pimm's No 1 with 3 parts lemonade. Mix well with a stirrer and add a sprig or two of fresh mint, some cucumber slices if you like and some fruit such as lemon, apple or orange slices or strawberries. Or even better on a hot afternoon prepare a large jug of Pimm's and take it into the garden to enjoy with friends.

There's something incredibly romantic about the notion of the traditional English picnic. It has an air of nostalgia about it, conjuring up images of wicker baskets filled to the brim with food and china laid out by the riverside on a lazy summer day. Embraced by English literature, the picnic makes for an idyllic scene: the rug on the grass, the pop of the cork and the clink of the glasses, and the feast laid out in all its glory. In my mind's eye the setting is the epitome of summer; shades of green woven into the landscape, sweet smelling grass, the gentle breeze lightly brushing my face and the occasional buzz of a bee in the flowers or the light flutter of a passing butterfly. The skies are always blue and the sun is always shining...

Of course, in reality, the English weather is changeable and unpredictable and you could just as easily be looking up at darkening skies, hastily packing away the picnic, before making a dash for the car. But on those rare and precious days when the skies are idyllically blue and the sun is shining triumphantly down oh, those are the days for a truly fabulous and memorable picnic.

*A peek inside my picnic hamper...*
* Plump black olives
* Sweet cherry tomatoes
* Parma ham
* Cold roast chicken
* A rocket salad
* Good cheese and fresh crusty bread
* Kentish strawberries
* Ripe figs

* Home-made lemonade (page 32)
* A bottle of Prosecco

If you decide to take a salad pack the dressing in a separate little container and drizzle it over just before you eat the salad. If you choose the Red apple and Parma Ham Salad pack the apples whole and slice them just before serving so that they don't turn brown.

Picnics don't have to be restricted to the summer months. September is often glorious with beautiful, golden sunshine. When the weather is still warm it's lovely to have an autumnal picnic, with ripe, seasonal food, as I did on the last weekend in September 2009. It was unseasonably hot so Rob and I took off in the car with our dog, Charlie, and picnicked in a field. We lay a blanket on the ground under the shade of a wise old tree and sat eating a Pear, Fig and Stichelton Salad (see page 103) as we watched the sun sink behind the tree-lined fields. What a celebration of autumn!

The following few pages feature some suggestions for perfect picnic recipes and there are also these good recipes dotted elsewhere:

* Asparagus, Avocado and
  Pea Shoot Salad (page 14)
* Jersey Royal Salad page 16)
* Red Apple and Parma Ham
  Salad (page 37)
* Home-made Lemonade (page 32)
* Apple and Raspberry Tart (page 41)
* Marinated Black Olives (page 96)
* Pear, Fig and Stichelton Salad
  (page 103)

# Smoked Salmon, Cream Cheese and Cress Wraps

Sandwiches on picnics can be fairly boring and they often suffer in transport. Tortilla wraps, on the other hand, are a little more interesting with less risk of sogginess. Once I've made them up I wrap them in baking parchment (which I keep them in as I eat them) and then wrap them again in foil to keep them fresh on the journey.

One of my favourite sandwiches in the world is smoked salmon and thickly spread cream cheese with a squeeze of fresh lemon juice. For picnics, and packed lunches, I like to make a version with wraps instead of bread, and lots of cress, which I've recently rediscovered. Poor old cress gets a bit of a rough deal. Unable to shake off the tarnish of retro salads and egg and cress sandwiches it's been banished from most people's kitchens, which is a shame because it has a great flavour and is good as an ingredient it its own right rather than just as a garnish.

**Makes 2 wraps**

80g cream cheese
2 tortilla wraps
4 slices smoked salmon
$1/_2$ lemon
1 handful cress
freshly ground black pepper,
    optional

Thickly spread half the cream cheese over half of each of the wraps. Season the cheese with a little black pepper if using. Lay 2 slices of smoked salmon over the cheese on each wrap and squeeze over some fresh lemon juice. Divide the cress between the two wraps and roll up the wraps. Cut the wraps in half to serve, if you like.

# Scotch Eggs

Home-made scotch eggs can be something of a revelation – or at least, they were for me the first time I made them. They seem to be something of a mystery but once you make them at home you'll see just how easy they are. Try them yourself and I'm certain you'll be converted from buying factory made ones; especially once you've eaten them warm straight from the pan while the coating is still crispy.

I like my eggs still a little squidgy in the middle and so I boil them for 7 minutes, but they are just as nice with a firmer yolk and, for a change, are quite lovely with a runny yolk – just make sure you put them on plates and use a knife to cut them open rather than bite into them and have yolk dripping everywhere!

You know this already, I'm sure, but I wouldn't be able to sleep at night if I didn't tell you to never, ever leave hot fat unattended – not for even a moment; it can go from being hot to catching alight in seconds. You should ideally use a thermostatic deep fat fryer but if using a frying pan keep a lid large enough to cover it close by to smother the flames should the oil catch light. Never throw water over burning oil.

**Makes 6 scotch eggs**

6 eggs
500g good quality pork sausages
a small handful of flat-leaf parsley, finely chopped
20g plain flour
1 egg, beaten
80g white breadcrumbs (see Cook's notes)
sunflower or vegetable oil, for deep frying
sea salt and freshly ground black pepper

Fill a medium pan with enough water to cover the eggs and bring it to the boil. When the water is boiling, carefully lower the eggs into the pan, using a slotted spoon. Gently simmer them for 6 minutes for a runny yolk, 7 minutes for a yolk that is firm but still a little soft in the middle, or 8 minutes for a just-set yolk. As soon as the cooking time is up immediately drain the eggs and place them under cold, running water to stop them from cooking any further. Peel them and set aside.

Place the flour, beaten egg and breadcrumbs into three small bowls.

Score the sausages lengthways through the skin and remove the meat. Put the sausagemeat into a medium mixing bowl, add the parsley, season well and stir well to combine. Divide the sausage mixture into 6 equal portions.

Take one portion of the sausagemeat, dust it with a little flour from the bowl it and pat it with your hands into a flat oval shape large enough to cover the egg. Put the egg into the centre and bring the sausagemeat around the egg, patting it together with your hands so that there are no gaps. It may seem like the meat will never go around the egg but keep working it with your hands and it will. It's important to make sure it's sealed well otherwise it will come apart when it cooks.

Next, dip the sausage-wrapped egg into the beaten egg to coat it. Then dip the wrapped egg into the breadcrumbs to cover it completely. Place the breadcrumb coated egg on a plate. Repeat for the other eggs.

If you don't have a deep fat fryer use a large, deep frying pan. If using a frying pan the amount of oil needed will depend on its size. For safety it should be filled no more than a third full with oil – remember it will rise when the eggs are added. Heat the oil until it is hot enough for a breadcrumb to turn golden in about 30 seconds. You don't want it any hotter or the breadcrumbs will brown too quickly and the sausagemeat won't cook through. If the oil starts to smoke it's too hot and at risk of catching light so immediately turn off the heat and let it cool down.

Carefully lower the eggs into the oil and cook them for about 10 minutes, turning so that they cook evenly, until the breadcrumbs are golden and the sausagemeat is cooked through.

If using a deep fat fryer heat the oil to 150°C and cook the eggs for about 8 minutes, carefully turning once or twice if the fat doesn't quite cover them.

Once the eggs are cooked carefully remove them with a slotted spoon and leave them to drain on kitchen paper.

Either serve the eggs warm or leave them to cool, then wrap them in baking parchment and put them in an airtight container and store in the fridge for up to 1 day.

**Cook's notes**
Making breadcrumbs is really easy and a great way of using up stale bread. All you need to do is simply break up some stale bread and process it in a food processor. Breadcrumbs freeze really well so you can make some with whatever stale bread you have and freeze them and then add to them each time you have a little leftover bread; better than throwing it away and handy to have in the freezer for recipes such as this.

I much prefer to buy pork sausages from the butchers and use the meat from them than buy sausagemeat separately as it never seems to taste as good.

# Chorizo and Tomato Tart

I love the combination of chorizo and tomatoes; they go together so well and are fantastic on this puff pastry tart with rocket. The tart can be eaten hot but when cold it makes great picnic food.

375g ready-rolled puff pastry
100g cooked chorizo, skinned
1–2 large tomatoes, preferably on the vine
1 egg, beaten, for glazing the pastry with (optional)
1 large handful rocket leaves

Preheat the oven to 200°C/ fan 180°C/gas mark 6. Line a large baking tray with baking parchment.

Place the pastry on the lined baking tray. Using a sharp knife, score lines around all four sides of the pastry, about 3cm from the edge, being careful not to cut all the way through. This will allow the edges to puff up nicely.

Slice the chorizo and tomatoes fairly finely and lay them over the middle of the pastry (in between the lines you've scored). For an optional glossy finish brush the edges of the pastry with a beaten egg.

Bake the tart in the oven for 15–20 minutes, until the pastry is golden then allow it to cool a little and scatter over the rocket leaves. Cut the tart into 4 and serve it warm or cold.

Rain is lashing down on this grey and miserable day in June, but as far as my tastebuds are concerned it's a gloriously hot summer's day. I'm eating ripe English strawberries; ~~and~~ the epitome of the British summer. Think of English strawberries and you'll think of strawberries and cream, Wimbledon, Eton Mess, strawberry jam.

Blog entry, June 2007

# Strawberries with White Balsamic Vinegar

You may have heard how balsamic vinegar is an incredible, if rather unlikely, match for strawberries, bringing out their delicious flavour. When I first came across a bottle of white balsamic vinegar at Borough market a few years ago I instantly knew it would be a fantastic hit with strawberries, being sweeter and milder than the darker variety – and so it was. I know balsamic vinegar with strawberries sounds odd but do try it; you'll be amazed at the difference it makes.

**Serves 4**

450g strawberries
1 tablespoon white balsamic
   vinegar
double cream, to serve

Either hull the strawberries or leave them as they are with their leafy tops intact and place in a serving bowl. Sprinkle the vinegar over the strawberries and toss them in it. Leave them to marinate for 20 minutes at room temperature.

Serve the strawberries at room temperature with double cream, lightly whipped if you prefer.

# If there's one thing the British love in the summertime it's a barbecue.

At the merest hint of a good weather weekend we're out stripping the supermarket shelves of sausages, chicken and burger buns. Rob and I love having a barbecue as much as the next couple and sometimes we'll even light it just for ourselves and sit out in the garden until late. In fact, we like doing that even when it's cold outside; we have a chiminea, which is just the right size to cook for two on and to sit around to keep warm. Rob's parents often have a barbecue on Bonfire Night, which is great fun too, so don't feel you have to wait for sunshine!

In the summer when we get a good weather weekend and we're making the barbecue into a bit of a party I like to decorate the garden with balloons and other decorations such as colourful windmills and paper flowers. As soon as the barbecue comes out we happily turn into complete stereotypes, with Rob doing his manly thing lighting the barbecue and taking charge of the sausages and me chopping away preparing colourful kebabs and salads. We fill buckets with ice to hold beer and wine and make up jugs of Pimm's full of fruit. We make a great team but no matter how prepared we think we are we usually end up serving up the food later than expected because time just flies past when we start greeting guests, chatting, getting drinks and doing last minute preparations. I always think 'Oh, I'll leave the chicken to marinade for a bit longer and make up the skewers just before they

need to go on,' or 'The burgers only take 5 minutes to mix up and pat together so I'll do it while the guests are chatting in the garden'. Then I end up rushing around trying to do everything at the last minute! Take my advice and prepare everything you can up front, even down to having plates and cutlery out, otherwise you'll end up running around and you won't be able to enjoy your own party.

When it comes to barbecue food you have so much choice. The trick is to scale down the selection you offer your guest and up the volume of that selection, rather than having a little of everything that doesn't come together very well. So, rather than offering up every kind of meat, seafood and side dish so your guests end up with confusing platefuls of mismatched food, choose just a handful and make them in large batches. You could even go for just one spectacular centrepiece to put on the barbecue such as a butterflied leg of lamb or a large whole salmon, wrapped in sheets of wet newspaper, as a neighbour of mine once did. The salmon was on the barbecue for about an hour and it cooked beautifully inside the paper. Now that was a memorable barbecue!

# Beef Burgers

Making your own burgers takes hardly any effort at all and yet is very gratifying. As you, and your friends, bite into tasty, juicy burgers sandwiched in a ciabatta roll with rocket leaves and Tomato Relish (see page 68) you'll marvel at the difference between home-made and shop-bought burgers and feel a sense of pride that you made them yourself.

Once you've made your own burgers you won't want to buy ready made ones again. You can make them exactly how you want and add to the mix whatever takes your fancy. And why not get the kids involved? They'll love making, and of course eating, their own burgers and you'll know exactly what's gone into them – the burgers, and the kids, that is!

**Makes 4 burgers**

500g good-quality beef mince
1 onion, finely diced
2 teaspoons Dijon mustard
1 handful flat-leaf parsley, finely
    chopped
olive oil or vegetable oil, for frying
sea salt and freshly ground black
    pepper
4 ciabatta rolls, rocket leaves and
    Tomato relish (page 68), to serve

Put the beef, onion, mustard and parsley into a large bowl, season it, and then mix it together with your hands. If you want to check the seasoning take a pinch of the mixture, fry it until it is cooked and then taste it.

Once you've mixed everything together you just need to firmly squeeze and mould the mixture into round patties. You can then fry them over a medium heat or cook them on the barbecue. Timings will depend on how thick you make the burgers and whether you fry or barbecue them, but as a guide they will need to be cooked for around 3–5 minutes on each side.

To serve, split the rolls and add a burger to each, top with relish and some rocket leaves.

**Cook's note**
Use the best quality mince you can find for your burgers and you'll be rewarded with succulence and fantastic flavour. When you have that good starting point anything you add is just going to enhance the flavour that's already there. To this recipe you could add crushed garlic, finely chopped chilli, different herbs or a strong-flavoured cheese such as mature Cheddar or Stilton in the middle of each burger. Some recipes suggest adding breadcrumbs or an egg to bind the mixture but I find I don't need to so long as I firmly squeeze the mixture together when moulding it.

**Lamb burgers**
Follow the recipe above replacing the beef mince with lamb mince, and the Dijon mustard and parsley with 1 deseeded and finely chopped medium red chilli and 2 tablespoons finely chopped mint.

# Tomato Relish

Making your own relish, chutney or jam is one of those activities that makes you feel particularly domesticated and virtuous. They're great to be able to pull out of the fridge and proudly add to meals for weeks to come.

**Makes approximately 500ml**

olive oil
1 onion, finely diced
2 garlic cloves, crushed
1kg ripe tomatoes, diced
3 or 4 sprigs fresh oregano, leaves stripped off or $1/2$ teaspoon dried oregano
100ml red wine vinegar
1–2 red or green chillies (see Cook's note), finely chopped
2 tablespoons caster sugar
sea salt and freshly ground black pepper

500ml glass preserving jar with a rubber sealing ring, sterilised (see Cook's notes)

Pour a little olive oil into a large pan set over a medium heat. Add the onion and garlic to the pan and sauté them for a couple of minutes. Add the remaining ingredients and season the mixture. Bring it up to the boil and then simmer it for about 45 minutes, stirring occasionally, until it's nice and thick.

Pour the hot relish into the hot sterilised preserving jar, secure the rubber ring in place and close the jar.

The relish will keep in the fridge for about a month. Once opened continue to store the relish in the fridge.

**Cook's notes**
You can make this relish as spicy or as mild as you like; I'll leave the amount, and choice, of chilli to you. Generally, the smaller the chilli the hotter it is so if you want to go easy start with one medium chilli and add more if you need to, or if you want to whack up the heat go for small bird's eye chillies. Remember that the heat is in the seeds and fibres so deseed the chillies first to reduce their fire, or leave them in for a real kick.

To sterilise the jar preheat the oven to 160°C/fan 140°F/gas mark 3. First check the jar is free from cracks or chips then wash it thoroughly in hot soapy water, rinse and dry it. Place the jar in the oven for 10 minutes. Then turn the oven off, leaving the jar inside until the relish is ready. To sterilise the rubber ring, submerge it in boiling water for at least 3 minutes and then leave it in the water until you are ready to pot the relish.

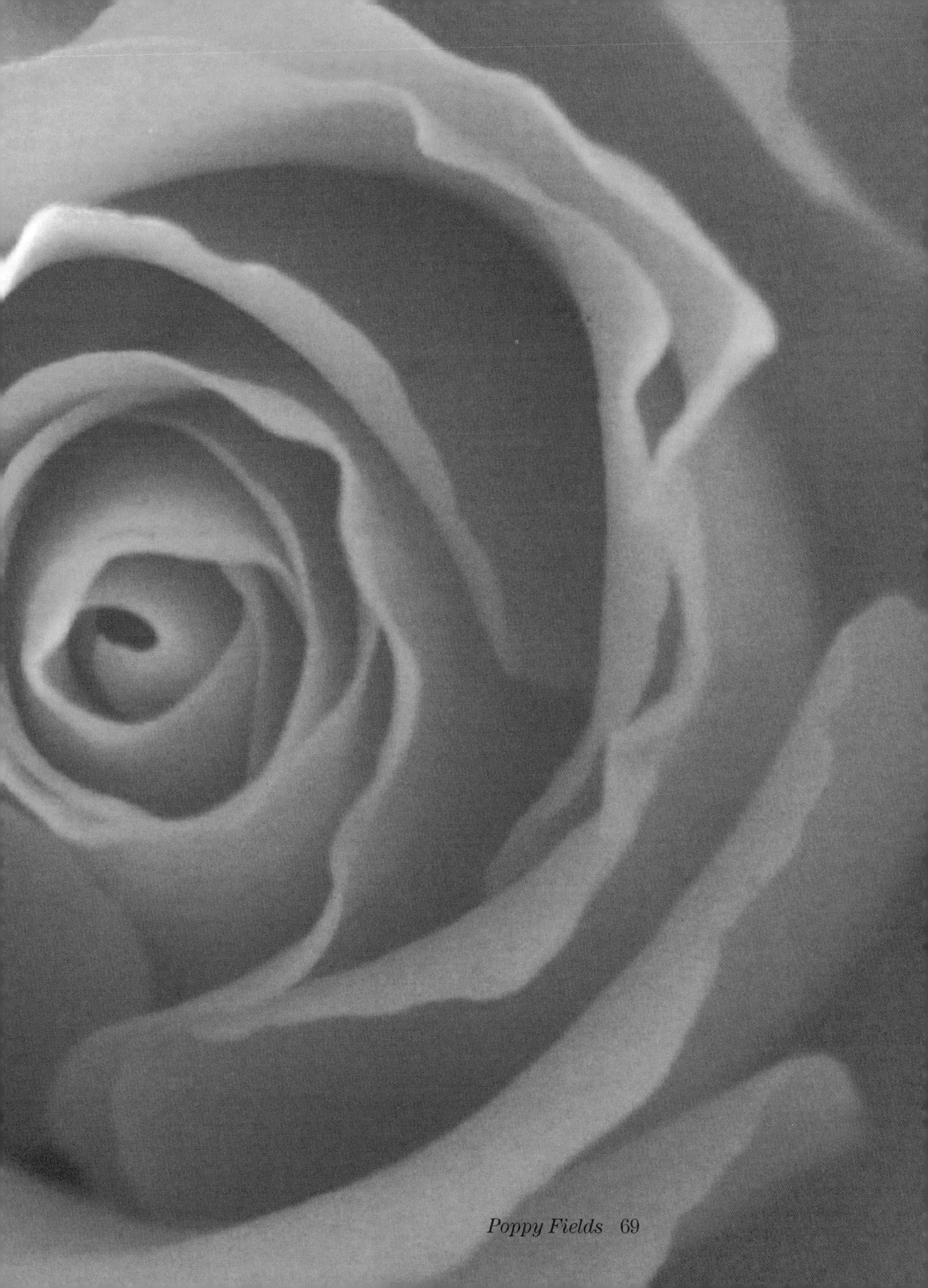

# Vegetable Skewers

These colourful skewers are a great addition to any barbecue and you can play around with the vegetables, adding whatever you like. Or why not put a selection of vegetables in dishes and let guests make their own pick 'n' mix skewers?

**Makes 6 skewers**

2 red onions, cut into bite-sized pieces
2 courgettes, cut into bite-sized pieces
1 red pepper, cut into bite-sized pieces
1 yellow pepper, cut into bite-sized pieces
olive oil, for brushing

6 wooden or metal skewers

If the skewers are wooden soak them in water for 15 minutes to prevent them from catching alight on the barbecue.

Push alternate pieces of vegetables onto the skewers, dividing them equally between all the skewers. Brush the vegetables with olive the oil. Cook the skewers for about 10 minutes on a hot barbecue or in a hot griddle pan, turning frequently until the vegetables are charred and softened.

# Chicken, Halloumi and Cherry Tomato Skewers

Halloumi cheese originates from Cyprus and is made from a mixture of goat's and sheep milk. It's a hard cheese, with a higher melting point than most cheeses so it's ideal for the barbecue. It's quite salty so you shouldn't need to add any more salt to these skewers but you might want to sprinkle over a little black pepper.

**Makes 6 skewers**

**For the marinade**
2 teaspoons paprika
2 tablespoons olive oil
1 garlic clove, crushed

**For the skewers**
2 skinless chicken breasts, cut into bite-sized pieces
250g halloumi cheese, cut into bite-sized cubes

18 cherry tomatoes, preferably on the vine
freshly ground black pepper (optional)

6 wooden or metal skewers

If the skewers are wooden soak them in water for 15 minutes to prevent them from catching alight on the barbecue.

Mix together the ingredients for the marinade in a medium non-metallic bowl then add the chicken pieces. Mix the chicken with the marinade so that it's well covered in it then cover the bowl with foil and leave the chicken to marinate in the fridge for at least 1 hour.

When you are ready to assemble the kebabs, push alternate pieces of chicken, cheese and then a whole tomato onto the skewers, dividing all the ingredients equally between the skewers.

Season the skewers with a little black pepper if you like, and then cook them on a hot barbecue or in a hot griddle pan, turning frequently, for about 15 minutes or until the chicken is cooked through and the juices run clear.

# The Parsons Family Coleslaw

Rob's mum, Carol, is a fantastic cook and is always throwing barbecues and family parties with lots of great food. This creamy coleslaw usually makes an appearance, much to my delight, and I pile it high on my plate. After years of scoffing it unabashedly I asked for the recipe so that I could make it myself. The recipe originally came from Rob's aunt Barbara, his dad's sister, who has been making it for years. She passed the recipe onto Carol, who passed it onto me and now I pass it onto you.

**Serves 6–8**

½ white cabbage, approximately
    400g
2 large carrots
1 small onion
4–6 tablespoons mayonnaise

Shred the cabbage, carrots and onions using a mandolin or food processor. Alternatively slice the cabbage and onions into thin strips using a sharp knife and grate the carrots.

Put the vegetables into a large bowl and mix them together with enough mayonnaise to bind the mixture and give you a consistency you're happy with. Cover and chill in the fridge until you are ready to serve. The coleslaw will keep for a couple of days in the fridge.

**Cook's notes**
Neither Carol nor Barbara use exact measures; they simply make the coleslaw by eye and by taste. But in order to give you an idea of the quantities I've given suggestions for the vegetables in the recipe. Do feel free to change the quantities as you prefer. Similarly with the mayonnaise; I tend to be quite generous with it but you can use as little or as much as you like – but however much you use the real trick is to use full-fat Hellman's!

# Warm Chive Potato Salad

*Potato salads are very easy to make; just boil some new potatoes, dress them in olive oil or mayonnaise and add whatever else to them you like: chopped shallots or garlic, a handful of chopped herbs, a sprinkling of lemon juice, chopped crispy bacon, green beans or peas – anything goes! The following are a couple of simple suggestions.*

**Serves 4 as a side dish**

500g new potatoes, left whole if
    very small or halved
approximately 10g chives
2 tablespoons extra virgin olive oil
sea salt

Put the potatoes in a large pan of salted water, bring to the boil and cook for 15–20 minutes or until tender.

Drain the potatoes and while they're still warm put them in a serving bowl, pour over the olive oil and toss well to coat. Use kitchen scissors to snip the chives into the bowl, add a good sprinkling of sea salt and toss everything together. Serve warm.

# Creamy Potato Salad

**Serves 4 as a side dish**

500g new potatoes, left whole if
    very small or halved
2 spring onions, finely sliced
2 tablespoons mayonnaise
2 or 3 handfuls of rocket
sea salt and freshly ground black
    pepper

Put the potatoes in a large pan of salted water, bring to the boil and cook for 15–20 minutes or until tender. Drain the potatoes and leave them to cool.

When the potatoes are cool put them into a large mixing bowl with the spring onions and mayonnaise. Season well and mix everything together.

Lay the rocket on a serving dish and top with the potatoes.

Post    Card

FOR CORRESPONDENCE        FOR ADDRESS ONLY

# pebbles and ice cream

I love seafood, and shellfish in particular is one of my favourite things in the world to eat. It always feels like such a treat to me, perhaps because, aside from the occasional retro prawn cocktail swathed in pink sauce, the shellfish of my childhood was experienced on family trips to the seaside, where we would eat cockles or prawns from little polystyrene cups, and so it brings the seaside that I love so much rushing back to me every time I eat it.

And just what is it that I love about the seaside? I don't think there's a short answer, I think it's a whole array of things, which, combined, make me feel such affection for it. Because I don't live near the sea, and never have, there's an element of escapism that appeals. As much as I like London it's nice to get away from the everyday hustle and bustle, and the minute the car hits the motorway headed south I feel my cares being carried away on the wind as it rushes through my hair from the open window. Even now, as an adult, it always feels like an exciting trip out with great things waiting at the end of the journey. As a child those things were sandcastles and paddling in the sea at Hastings on trips with my grandparents, and discovering crabs, seaweed and pretty shells on school trips; as a teenager they were B&Bs and bars in Brighton; and as an adult they are salty sea air and oysters in Whitstable.

One of the things I find so endearing about the seaside is its sheer Britishness. A big part of our identity and history is embedded in the seaside, a history that takes us on a nostalgic trip down memory lane where we find Punch and Judy, saucy postcards, fortune tellers and donkey rides. It's the place to go when the sun is shining; at the merest hint of a hot, sunny weekend or Bank Holiday, thousands of us rush to our cars and flock to Britain's coasts, only to sit for hours in queues of traffic on the motorway and then drive round in circles at our destination trying to find a car parking space! But when we do eventually escape the car and claim our tiny spot on the beach the pain of the journey evaporates – we're at the seaside! Even if the weather lets us down, as it so often does, we Brits make the most of every minute and won't let it spoil our fun. And what fun! Sticks of stripy rock wrapped in cellophane, slot machines and teddy-grab games on the pier, cafés and seafood stalls, 99 ice creams and deckchairs. OK, so it may lack style, but it will always have a place in the hearts of the British.

Of course one of the great lures of the seaside for me is the food – certainly that's what brings me back to Whitstable time and again. Those oysters! Oh, my! The first time I ever ate an oyster was at Whitstable, and where better for a first taste than in a town so renowned for them? Eating them is like throwing yourself into the sea and feeling the cool, salty waves wash over you; they're quite incredible. It's not only the oysters that are good at Whitstable; Rob and I quite often drive down there to pick up fresh fish for dinner from the fish market. It's great to be able to choose from the selection the boats have brought in that morning and then bring the fish home to cook, simply with just a few herbs, a drizzle of olive oil and perhaps some slices of lemon.

For food to enjoy while you're at the seaside you can't beat the golden-battered fish and chips that always seem to taste so much nicer there. I don't think there's a greater way of eating hot, salty chips than straight from the wrapper on a cold winter's day by the sea front. Even better if it starts to rain and you take shelter in one of those covered benches and look out to sea whilst popping steaming, slightly too-hot chips into your mouth and jiggling them around to avoid burning your tongue!

One of the things I love the most about the seaside is the effect the sea has on my mind and my sense of well being: it's so soothing and therapeutic. The waves gently caressing the pebbles on the beach still the mind and the fresh air calms as it's breathed in. But as well as relaxing the senses the sea can just as easily excite them. In tune with the weather, it can not only be still but it can be violent, and this can have just a positive an effect on the spirit as when it's calm; waves crashing against rocks on a dark and stormy day can be stimulating and clarifying for the mind.

Whatever it is that brings you to the seaside, you can be sure that when you leave to go home, sun sinking into the sea, white light reflecting off the rippling water in your rear view mirror as you say goodbye, it will stay in your memory for a lifetime.

# Baked Sea Bass with Spinach and Sautéed Potatoes

Sea bass is my favourite of all fish and I like to cook it very simply to allow its beautiful flavour to shine through. A few slices of lemon and a bay leaf is all that it needs. Cooking bass – any fish, in fact – in a foil parcel, as here, allows it to steam gently leaving the flesh deliciously succulent.

I like to serve spinach with the bass and perhaps a few sautéed potatoes or boiled new potatoes.

**Serves 2**

1 whole sea bass, approximately
    1kg, cleaned, scaled and gutted
1 lemon, thickly sliced
1 bay leaf
sea salt and freshly ground black
    pepper

**For the sautéed potatoes**
2 large potatoes, peeled and sliced
    approximately 1cm thick.
olive oil

**For the spinach**
a knob of butter
100g spinach

Preheat the oven to 200°C/
fan 180°C/gas mark 6.

Stuff the cavity of the bass with lemon slices and a bay leaf and season it all over. Fold a 100cm long piece of foil in half widthways. Lay the fish on the double-folded foil and bring the ends up together to form a loosely wrapped parcel. Place the foil-wrapped fish onto a baking tray. Bake the bass for about 30 minutes, or until cooked through. When the fish is cooked the flesh should be opaque and easily come away from the bone.

Bring a large pan of salted water to the boil and add the potato slices. Boil the slices for about 5 minutes, until they're almost, but not completely, cooked through and then drain them immediately, so that they don't break up in the water.

Drizzle some olive oil into a large frying pan and heat it over a high heat. Season the cooked potato slices then add a single layer of potatoes to the pan (you will probably need to do this in two batches). Sauté the potatoes, turning halfway through, until golden on both sides. If cooking in batches, keep the first half hot in the oven while you cook the remaining slices and then pop them in the oven too.

To cook the spinach, melt the butter over a medium heat, in the same pan the potatoes were cooked in, add the spinach and sauté it for a few minutes until it wilts. Squeeze the excess liquid out of the spinach and season it. To serve, place the fish, spinach and potatoes on a plate and serve straight away.

# King Prawn Linguine

This dish uses classic ingredients to complement the prawns: lemon, chilli and parsley. When you toss them all together their fragrances travel on the steam from the linguine to form a heady, aromatic cloud. It's a great dish for a casual lunch, served with a good bottle of chilled, dry white wine.

**Serves 4**

500g raw king prawns, peeled
320g dried linguine
olive oil
2 medium red chillies, deseeded
  and finely chopped
juice of 1 lemon
a handful flat-leaf parsley, chopped
sea salt and freshly ground black
  pepper

Devein the prawns by making an incision down their spines using a sharp knife and pulling out the black intestinal tract.

Bring a large pan of salted water to the boil then add the linguine. Bring the water back up to the boil and cook the pasta according to the pack instructions, until al dente – soft on the outside but still a little firm in the middle.

While the pasta is cooking heat the olive oil in a large frying pan then add the chillies and fry them for a minute over a medium heat. Add the prawns and fry them with the chilli for 2–3 minutes or until they turn completely pink. Once they're cooked remove the pan from the heat and stir in the lemon juice.

Add the linguine to the frying pan and toss everything together. Check the seasoning and add some sea salt and black pepper if necessary. Finally, sprinkle over the parsley and serve straight away.

# Mussels with Saffron and Capellini

This fragrant dish is rather difficult to eat with any finesse – all that capellini swimming in the infused broth makes for much messiness! My advice is not to bother trying but instead give yourself over to the sloppy slurpiness in the bowl – you'll enjoy it all the more.

**Serves 2**

150g dried capellini (see Cook's note)
a knob of butter
$\frac{1}{2}$ shallot, finely diced
pinch saffron strands
3 tablespoons dry white wine
500g mussels, cleaned (see Cook's note, page 81)
sea salt
crusty bread, to serve

Bring a large pan of salted water to the boil then add the capellini. Bring the water back up to the boil and cook the pasta according to the pack instructions, until al dente – soft on the outside but still a little firm in the middle.

While the capellini is cooking melt the butter in a large pan then add the shallot and sauté it for a few minutes. Turn the heat right up and add the saffron strands, the white wine and the mussels. Cover the pan with a lid and cook the mussels for 3–4 minutes, shaking the pan every now and then, until all the mussels have opened. Discard any that don't open and then add the cooked capellini to the mussels and broth.

Divide between two bowls and serve with crusty bread.

**Cook's note**
Capellini, which also goes by the delightful name of Angel Hair, is a finer version of spaghetti. If you can't get hold of it spaghetti or linguine will work just as well.

# Mussels in White Wine

My first experience of mussels was when I was 19 and working in central London for the first time – all grown up! A colleague took me out for lunch one day and ordered them, and when she heard I'd never tried them she urged me to do so, telling me how wonderful they are. I duly did and when they arrived I took in their plump forms sitting in gleaming black shells surrounded by winey, garlicky juices with wide eyes. I devoured them and mopped up the delicious juices with bread. Right there and then a life-long love of mussels began.

**Serves 2**

a knob of butter
1 shallot, finely diced
1 garlic clove, crushed
100ml dry white wine
1kg mussels, cleaned (see Cook's note)
3 tablespoons double cream (optional)
a small bunch of flat-leaf parsley, finely chopped
crusty bread, to serve

Melt the butter in a large pan then add the shallot and garlic, and sauté them over a medium heat for a few minutes until the shallot has softened. Add the white wine to the pan followed by the mussels. Put a lid on the pan and increase the heat to high. Cook the mussels for 3–4 minutes, shaking the pan now and then to move them around, until they've all opened. Discard any mussels that don't open at all.

Stir in the cream, if using, and sprinkle over the parsley before serving with crusty bread.

**Cook's note**
Clean the mussels well, scrubbing off any barnacles and pulling out the beards (the threads that protrude from between the shells). The rule for mussels is simple: before cooking discard any that are open and don't close when you tap them, and after cooking discard any that remain closed. You should also throw away any that have broken or damaged shells.

# Fish Pie

Fish pie is so comforting and delicious, it's perfect for putting on the table for family and friends to tuck into when the weather turns colder and the nights start to draw in.

Steamed green beans are a great accompaniment to fish pie, giving contrasting texture and flavour. And a good bottle of white wine is surely essential?

**Serves 4**

**For the topping**
1kg floury potatoes such as Maris Piper, peeled and cut into equal-sized chunks
50g butter
sea salt

**For the filing**
800g skinned and filleted firm-fleshed mixed fish (see Cook's note)
a knob of butter
1 leek, white and light green parts finely sliced
2 shallots, finely chopped
200ml double cream

100ml dry white wine
juice of $\frac{1}{2}$ lemon
1 bay leaf
a large handful of flat-leaf parsley, finely chopped
50g Parmesan cheese, grated
sea salt
freshly ground black pepper

Preheat the oven to 190°C/ fan 170°C/gas mark 5.

Put the potatoes in a large pan of salted water, bring to the boil and cook for 15–20 minutes or until tender. Drain and mash the cooked potatoes with the butter. Set the mashed potato aside.

Remove any bones from the fish, chop it into bite-sized pieces and place them in a medium ovenproof dish.

Melt the butter in a medium pan over a medium heat then add the leek and shallots and sauté them until softened. Next, add the cream, wine, lemon juice and bay leaf. Bring the mixture to the boil and

simmer it for about 15 minutes, stirring occasionally, until it thickens to a sauce-like consistency. At this stage turn off the heat and remove the bay leaf, then stir the parsley and cheese into the sauce. Season well and pour the sauce over the fish in the dish.

Top the fish with the mashed potato. Run a fork over the top horizontally and vertically for decoration and to help the crisp the top up in the oven. Bake the pie for 30–40 minutes, until the mashed potato is golden and the sauce underneath bubbling.

**Cook's note**
It doesn't really matter what fish you put into the pie so long as it's firm-fleshed and flavoursome, and responsibly fished from a sustainable source. I particularly like a simple mixture of cod and undyed smoked or unsmoked haddock but pollack, monkfish or salmon are all good to use too. For some added luxury add raw prawns or scallops to the mixed fish when you put it into the dish.

*The sea is calm tonight.*
*The tide is full, the moon lies fair*
*Upon the straits; on the French coast the light*
*Gleams and is gone; the cliffs of England stand,*
*Glimmering and vast, out in the tranquil bay.*
*Come to the window, sweet is the night air!*
*Only, from the long line of spray*
*Where the sea meets the moon-blanched land,*

*Listen! you hear the grating roar*
*Of pebbles which the waves draw back, and fling,*
*At their return, up the high strand,*
*Begin, and cease, and then again begin,*
*With tremulous cadence slow, and bring*
*The eternal note of sadness in.*

**Dover Beach**, Matthew Arnold

# Poached Salmon with Watercress and Chargrilled Cherry Tomatoes

This is a lovely dish that lets the ingredients do the talking. The gently poached salmon is wonderfully tender and flavoursome, complemented by the fresh watercress and sweet cherry tomatoes. A drizzle of good quality extra virgin olive oil and a sprinkling of sea salt is all the dressing it needs.

**Serves 4**

4 salmon fillets, skinned
4 bunches of cherry tomatoes on the vine, approximately 6 tomatoes on each
200g watercress
extra virgin olive oil
sea salt

Fill a deep frying pan, large enough to hold the salmon fillets, with salted water. Bring it to the boil and then add the salmon fillets. Bring the water to a barely a simmer, with just a few occasional bubbles coming to the surface, and poach the salmon until just cooked through. The cooking time will depend on the size and thickness of the fillets. As a guide, an average-sized fillet will take about 6–8 minutes. Check the salmon after about 5 minutes to see how much longer you think they'll need. The salmon is cooked when it just starts to flake when tested with a fork but will still be darker pink in the centre of the fillet. Remove the fillets from the water as soon as they're cooked to avoid them over-cooking.

While the salmon is cooking heat a griddle pan over a high heat. Add the tomatoes (there's no need for any oil), still on their vines, and cook them for about 5 minutes, until they're charred but not collapsed.

Pile the watercress onto plates along with the salmon and cherry tomatoes. Drizzle over a little extra virgin olive oil and sprinkle over a little sea salt.

**Cook's note**
Salmon should be just-cooked and have a slightly darker pink tinge in the middle; over-cooked fish will become rubbery and lose its fresh taste. When you gently poach salmon it's easy to control how far it's cooked and you can return it to the gently simmering water if necessary. It's important to keep the poaching liquid just barely simmering, so that the fish doesn't over-cook or break up.

# Filo Crab Parcels

These little crab-filled parcels make great canapés for a party or you could serve them as a starter with a little rocket – two or three parcels each will be plenty. They're as nice cold as they are warm but they're so tempting it's unlikely that they'll be around long enough to cool down!

**Makes 12 parcels**

6 sheets filo pastry, approximately 37 x 28cm (see Cook's note)
50g butter, melted

**For the filling**
200g white crab meat
1–2 medium red chillies, deseeded and finely chopped
2 spring onions, finely chopped
freshly squeezed lime juice, to taste
Approximately 2 tablespoons mayonnaise, to bind
sea salt and freshly ground black pepper

sweet chilli dipping sauce, to serve

Preheat the oven to 200°C/ fan 180°C/gas mark 6.

Mix all the filling ingredients together in a medium mixing bowl and season well. Taste it to make sure you're happy with the balance of flavours and add more lime juice, chilli or seasoning if necessary, then set it aside.

Cut each sheet of pastry into 4 squares approximately 12 x 12cm. Don't worry about being exact about this; you just need to make sure the squares are large enough to hold a tablespoon of the filling in a parcel. Cover the pastry with a damp tea towel to prevent it from drying out.

Using a pastry brush carefully dab one of the pastry squares with the melted butter (I find it easier to dab rather than brush and this is less likely to split the pastry) and place another square directly on top. Spoon about a tablespoon of the filling into the centre then pull the edges of the pastry up to the middle and squeeze them together so that you have a little parcel. Dab it all over with the butter. Repeat with the remaining pastry and filling.

Place the parcels onto a large non-stick baking tray and bake them for 10–12 minutes, until the pastry is golden. If necessary bake the parcels in batches or on two baking trays. Transfer to a wire rack to cool.

**Cook's note**
Take care to handle the pastry carefully or it will split and the filling will come out during cooking. It's worth having a few extra squares of pastry to wrap the parcels in if the pastry does split.

# Warm Bacon and Scallop Salad

Scallops always seem like a little luxury and a real treat to me. They go fabulously with bacon; its smokiness complements the sweetness of the tender scallops so well.

**Serves 2**

2 handfuls of salad leaves, e.g. lollo rosso, frisée or a mixture of baby leaves
1 rasher back bacon, roughly diced
a knob of butter
8 scallops
3–4 tablespoons white wine
sea salt and freshly ground black pepper

Arrange the salad leaves on 2 plates.

Fry the bacon in a medium non-stick frying pan until cooked then remove it from the pan. Add the butter to the pan then season the scallops and sear them for about 30 seconds on each side over a high heat. Remove them and lay them on the salad leaves with the bacon.

Slosh a little white wine into the pan to deglaze it, stirring it with a wooden spoon while it reduces, scraping all the bacon bits from the pan. When the wine has turned syrupy, drizzle it over the salad and serve immediately.

I simply adore lobster; the king of the shellfish. Eating it outside on a warm summer's day with a large dollop of mayonnaise and a glass of chilled white wine, perhaps with a few thin, salted chips, is surely a little piece of heaven on earth.

As a meat eater I'm comfortable with the concept of animals and fish as food. But, like many people in Britain, I've had my eyes opened in recent years by documentaries and reports about how animals are kept. I'm much more aware of the cradle to grave process than I used to be and try to buy meat that's come from animals reared with their welfare in mind. But the truth is, while I may think about the animal's welfare along the production line, I don't need to think too much about its slaughter; I pick the meat up from my butcher and that's it, someone else has done the rest for me. But with lobsters it's a different matter; they have to be cooked live or immediately after dispatch because, like all crustaceans, they deteriorate rapidly. For the same reason it's preferable to cook a lobster yourself rather than buy a ready cooked one as the texture of the flesh changes very quickly once cooked.

If I'm totally honest, dispatching a lobster is something I'd rather not have to do but if I want to cook it myself then I have to. But also, being a keen cook and food lover, I don't think I should just close my eyes to the reality of the preparation of meat and seafood, and if I'm prepared to go into a restaurant and have someone kill a lobster for me to eat shouldn't I be prepared to do it myself?

Now, I wouldn't go as far as to apply this argument to other animals, such as the slaughtering of pigs, for example, because firstly they're much larger and the dispatch is more complex and – most importantly – I'm untrained, and secondly I don't need to do it myself in order to cook it, as pork doesn't have to be eaten straight away after slaughter. But a lobster, on the other hand, is something that I am able to dispatch (with a little research and knowledge) and have to if I want to cook it myself at home.

Having had this debate go round my head for sometime, I finally took the bull by the horns, or rather, the lobster by the claws (sorry), and decided to buy a live lobster to cook myself. I'm not going to pretend that it was an easy thing to do; I battled with my nerves all the way to down to Whitstable – where I went to pick up the lobster – all the way back, and through every step of the process. I wanted to be absolutely certain that I was going to dispatch the lobster as humanely and correctly as I possibly could and so I researched the best way on the internet and by reading my cookbooks. Through this research I chose to put the lobster into the freezer to send it to sleep first, which is the recommendation of Rick Stein and Hugh Fearnley-Whittingstall, whose books (Rick Stein's *Seafood* and *The River Cottage Fish Book*) I turned to for advice on the subject.

The hardest part of the process for me was, perhaps surprisingly, not actually putting the lobster into the pot – although this was more than a little scary and I had to muster up some courage to do it, I knew that at that stage the lobster would know nothing about it, having been rendered unconscious by the freezer. No, the hardest part was the pang of guilt I felt when I closed the freezer door on the lobster. I think in order to deal with this you really have to make the shift in your mind to thinking of the lobster, simply, as food.

But now that I've passed that first-time hurdle (which you can read the full account of on my blog) I feel more comfortable with cooking lobster. I have since cooked it again and will do so in the future. It does get easier and, aside from enabling you to have an incredibly delicious meal at home, cooking lobster yourself makes you appreciate, and respect, it all the more. And it really brings home the importance of the welfare of the animals that feed us, right from their very beginnings to their very ends, and of responsible production lines of the meat and seafood that we eat.

# Lobster

1 lobster (ask the fishmonger to
     weigh it for you)
salt (25g per litre of water)
thin chips and mayonnaise,
     to serve

First put the lobster into a freezer
for 2 hours, which will send it into
a deep sleep. If you need to weigh
the lobster yourself, now is the
time to do it, after it has been in the
freezer.

Next, you need to work out how long
to cook it for, which is 15 minutes
if it weighs up to 700g, or 20 minutes
up to 1.5kg.

When you're ready to cook the
lobster fill a pan large enough for
you to fully submerge it in water,
measure the water in litres as you
go so you know how much salt to
add. Next, add 25g salt per litre of
water. Bring the water to the boil
and when it's rapidly boiling put
the lobster into the water quickly
and fully; there can be no
hesitation here. Once the lobster is
fully submerged pop a lid onto the
pot and bring the water back up to
the boil. Cook the lobster for the
length of time calculated according
to its weight. It will turn a stunning
shade of coral as it cooks.

To serve the lobster place it belly
down on a chopping board with its
head facing you. Put the tip of a
sharp knife into the middle of the
head then cut down firmly in a
straight line right down the centre
until you hit the board. Next, turn
the lobster around and follow the
same line with the knife right down
the body and through the tail –
you'll need a bit of force for this.
Discard the stomach sac (which is
in the head), the gills, and the black
intestinal tract in the tail. The
greeny-brown liver is perfectly
edible and rich tasting.

Serve the lobster in its shell, with
seafood crackers to get the meat
out of the claws, thin chips and
plenty of mayonnaise.

# Vanilla Ice Cream

This is a custard-based ice cream made, simply, by churning sweeter than usual rich custard in an ice cream maker. The custard base makes for a deliciously creamy ice cream; the stuff that dreams are made of.

1 vanilla pod
350ml full fat milk
250ml double cream
5 egg yolks
90g caster sugar
1 teaspoon cornflour

**Makes approximately 700ml**

Split the vanilla pod lengthways with a sharp knife, and then run the back of the knife along the inside of the pod to remove the seeds. Put the seeds and pod into a medium non-stick pan with the milk and cream then heat the mixture to just below boiling point – when steam starts to rise from the pan.

Place the egg yolks, sugar and cornflour in a large bowl and whisk them together until the mixture is pale yellow. Stir the milk and cream into the egg and sugar mixture, and then pour it into a clean medium non-stick pan. Add the vanilla pod to the pan then heat the mixture gently until it thickens, stirring all the time with a wooden spoon. Don't allow it to boil. Remove the vanilla pod then pour the custard into a bowl and leave it to cool down completely.

Once cool, pour the custard into an ice cream maker and churn it according to the manufacturer's instructions.

*Once you've mastered the basic vanilla ice cream try any of the following different flavours.*

## Marshmallow and chocolate chip ice cream

Follow the recipe for vanilla ice cream and after churning remove it from the ice cream maker to allow it to soften a little. Then mix in 100g chocolate chips and 50g roughly chopped marshmallows.

## Chocolate orange ice cream

Break up 100g 70% cocoa solids dark chocolate into pieces and place it in a small heatproof bowl. Fill a small pan about a quarter full with water and bring it to the boil. Put the bowl over the pan of water, making sure the base doesn't touch the water. The steam will gently melt the chocolate. Check occasionally to ensure the pan doesn't boil dry. Follow the recipe for vanilla ice cream and add the zest of 2 oranges to the cream and milk. Once the custard has thickened and you've poured it into a bowl whisk in the melted chocolate and the juice of 1–2 oranges according to taste. Leave the mixture to cool then churn it in an ice cream maker.

## Summer berry ice cream

Heat 150g fresh or frozen summer berries with 2 tablespoons icing sugar in a small pan until the berries break down and form a sauce. Mashing them with a fork as they cook helps this process. Strain the sauce through a sieve then allow it to cool. Follow the recipe for vanilla ice cream and after churning remove it from the ice cream maker to allow it to soften a little. Then lightly fold the sauce in, making a ripple effect.

## Cook's note

Fresh berries are great to use when they're in season, but it's handy to keep a bag of frozen berries in the freezer for desserts such as this.

# Strawberry and Clotted Cream Ice Cream

This is quite literally traditional strawberries and cream in the form of ice cream. Fruity, rich, creamy and indulgent it's an ideal after dinner dessert. Not only is it incredibly simple to make but the real beauty of it is that you don't need to make a custard base first and you don't need an ice cream maker, as the cream gives it a perfect texture with no need for whisking as it sets. You can just put it in the freezer and forget about it until it's ready – perfect!

**Serves 4**

450g strawberries, hulled
200g clotted cream
150g caster sugar
whole unhulled strawberries,
   to decorate
wafer biscuits, to serve (optional)

Blend the strawberries with the cream and sugar in a blender or food processor until smooth.

Pour the mixture into a freezerproof plastic container and freeze for approximately 7 hours or until set. Take it out of the freezer to allow it to soften up before serving with wafer biscuits, if you like.

# Raspberry and Mint Sorbet

The idea for this sorbet came to me from a rather fabulous frozen Raspberry Mojito cocktail I once had in a London bar. As I discovered, raspberry and mint is an astonishing combination, and together they make for a very fruity and refreshing sorbet, stunningly vivid in both colour and flavour. Eat it on a scorching hot day – it's like summer intensified.

**Serves 4**

1kg raspberries
300g caster sugar
2 tablespoons finely chopped mint
3 tablespoons raspberry liqueur,
   such as Chambord (optional)
fresh mint leaves and whole
   raspberries, to decorate

Place the raspberries and sugar in a large pan and heat them very gently until the sugar dissolves and the raspberries break down. Remove the pan from the heat and pass it through a sieve to remove the seeds. Add the mint and liqueur, if using, to the raspberry mixture, stir well and then allow it to cool.

Once the mixture is cool, stir it thoroughly then churn it in an ice cream maker according to the manufacturer's instructions. If you haven't got an ice cream maker pour the mixture into a freezerproof plastic container and put it in the freezer. Mix the sorbet with a fork or whisk about every 3 hours as it freezes to break down any ice crystals that form. It will take about 10 hours to freeze completely.

Serve scoops of the sorbet decorated with fresh mint leaves and whole raspberries.

# linen and tea roses

Food is best when shared. Much of the pleasure of cooking is in making meals for other people, and gathering friends around the table and enjoying good food and flowing wine is one of the greatest joys in life. When you invite friends for lunch or dinner you want it to be an enjoyable time for everyone, including yourself. A little advance planning and familiarisation with what you intend to cook will help to ensure that it is.

As I spend so much of my time developing recipes I often try them out on my family when I invite them over for a meal. My poor family have got used to being guinea pigs and I'm fortunate that they're patient and understanding, even when things don't quite go according to plan! But trying out a new dish for the first time on guests is not a course of action I would ordinarily recommend. If you want your guests to be relaxed then you need to be relaxed, which is not going to happen if you're trying to cook an unfamiliar dish and worrying how it will turn out. So choose a dish you know well or, if you do want to try something new, practise it in advance. At the very least familiarise yourself with the recipe, know what you need to do when and have everything to

hand, including the right pans and utensils. Where possible prepare as much as you can beforehand to save time and trouble later. Can you prepare the vegetables, make the puddings, plate up and refrigerate the starters? Obviously some foods won't sit around for too long without starting to spoil, so do bear this in mind, but peeled potatoes and carrots, for example, will wait quite happily in pans filled with water, ready to simply put on the hob, for several hours. Other things you can do in advance are setting the table, including plates and glasses, taking serving dishes out of the cupboards so you have them to hand, plating up desserts, if you have room in the fridge. And don't forget to chill the wine!

One the most difficult things when entertaining is getting the timings right. Making sure everything is cooked,hot and ready to be served up can be challenging at the best of times, but when you have guests who you're trying to chat to in between dashing in and out of the kitchen it can really be quite tricky. My friends Julie and Steve have never let me forget the time I served them a roast chicken

meal with nicely cooked chicken, crispy roast potatoes, sweet carrots and rock-hard cauliflower you could have played cricket with. Oh yes, many a time I've willed the water to boil and the oven to cook quicker whilst telling people dinner will only be (another) 10 minutes! When it comes to entertaining planning really is everything, so work out your timings in advance. I should add that I don't always take my own advice here. Which is probably why I sometimes serve up cricket balls instead of cauliflower.

# Marinated Black Olives

Marinated olives are quick and easy to make and are great to offer guests with drinks. I use black olives because I personally prefer them but you could use green or a mixture. Experiment with different ingredients for the marinade: try different vinegars (or none), lemon zest or finely chopped chilli. Cubes of feta cheese and/or roasted red peppers are also nice additions.

**Serves 8**

200g black pitted or unpitted olives, drained

**For the marinade**
2 tablespoons extra virgin olive oil
2 teaspoons red wine vinegar
1–2 garlic cloves, sliced into thin slivers
2 sprigs thyme or 1 sprig rosemary (or a mixture), leaves stripped off and finely chopped

Put all the marinade ingredients into a medium mixing bowl and mix them together. Add the olives and toss them in the marinade so that they're thoroughly coated. Leave them to marinate at room temperature for at least an hour, but the longer the better. Serve the olives at room temperature.

The olives will keep for a few days in the fridge in an airtight container if you are not serving them immediately, but remember to let them come to room temperature before serving,

# Parma Ham-wrapped Avocado Slices

These simple canapés are great to serve with drinks on a summer evening.

**Makes 16 canapés**

2 ripe avocados, halved and stoned
8 slices Parma ham
sea salt

Slice each avocado half lengthways into four pieces then peel off the skin. If you like you can sprinkle over a little sea salt but you'll only need a very small amount as Parma ham can be fairly salty.

Cut each slice of Parma ham into two and wrap one piece around each slice of avocado. Secure with cocktail sticks and place on a serving plate.

# Cheesy Garlic Bread

Everyone loves garlic bread and it's the perfect thing to pass around and share, whether as a starter or as a side to the main meal.

**Serves 4**

60g butter, softened
2 garlic cloves, crushed
1 handful flat-leaf parsley, chopped
1 ciabatta loaf or 1 French stick
60g mature Cheddar cheese, grated

Preheat the oven to
200°C/180°C/gas mark 6

Place the butter, garlic and parsley in a small bowl and mash it together using a fork.

If using ciabatta cut it in half lengthways then again widthways to make four pieces. Spread the butter over each piece then sprinkle over the cheese.

Place the bread on a non-stick baking tray and bake it for about 10 minutes, until the cheese has melted and the bread is golden.

If using a French stick slice it as though you are cutting it into rounds, but don't cut right through to the bottom, so that the stick still remains in one piece, and then stuff the butter and cheese between each cut.

Wrap the bread loosely in foil then place it on a baking tray. Bake it for 8 minutes then open up the foil and bake it for about 5 minutes more, until it turns golden.

**Cook's note**
If the French stick is very large you may want to double quantity of garlic butter and cheese.

# Cheese Straws

Cheese straws are great for passing around with drinks and you can have lots of fun coming up with different types to make.

**Makes at least 30 straws**

**Basic cheese straws**
375g ready-rolled puff pastry
2 large handfuls of good strong
  Cheddar or Parmesan cheese,
  grated
1 egg, beaten (optional)

Preheat the oven to 200°C/ fan 180°C/gas mark 6. Line a large baking tray with baking parchment.

Lay the pastry on a floured worksurface with the long sides facing you. Lightly score a line lengthways down the centre of the pastry and sprinkle the cheese lengthways across one half of the marked pastry. Brush the edges of the pastry with cold water, to help them stick together. Bring the uncovered half of the pastry down over the bottom along the scored line so that it's folded in half lengthways with the cheese sandwiched in between.

Gently roll a rolling pin over the pastry to press it together well, and then cut it into strips $1/2$–1 cm wide. Twist the strips quite tightly, but carefully to avoid breaking them. You can gently stretch them out a little to make them longer if you like.

Place some of the straws on the prepared tray until it is full, spacing them out well, as they will expand as they cook. If you like you can brush them with beaten egg to give them a nice glaze. Bake the straws, in batches, for 10–15 minutes, until golden. Transfer to a wire rack to cool.

**Variations**
Theses are a couple of my favourite alternatives to the basic recipe.

**Cheese and Marmite straws**
Follow the recipe for basic cheese straws as above, but spread the pastry with Marmite before sprinkling over the cheese. If you like, you can sprinkle over an extra handful of grated Cheddar or Parmesan cheese before baking.

**Parmesan and poppy seed straws**
Follow the recipe for basic cheese straws as above using Parmesan cheese and sprinkle the pastry with 1 teaspoon of poppy seeds, gently pressing them into the pastry, before cutting it into strips and twisting.

**Cook's note**
If you like you could use sesame seeds instead of, or as well as, the poppy seeds.

# Lamb Shanks Braised in Red Wine

The shank is a delicious cut of lamb that needs just a little love and some long, slow cooking to make it melt with tenderness.

olive oil
4 lamb shanks
2 celery sticks, roughly chopped
4 shallots or 1 small onion, diced
2 carrots, roughly chopped
2 garlic cloves, sliced
1 tablespoon plain flour
375ml red wine
200ml lamb or beef stock
2 sprigs thyme
1 bay leaf
sea salt and freshly ground black
    pepper
mashed potatoes, to serve

**Serves 4**

Preheat the oven to 150°C/ fan 130°C/gas mark 2.

Drizzle some olive oil into a large flameproof casserole dish and heat it over a high heat. Add the shanks to the dish and brown them all over (you may need to do this in batches), then remove and set them aside.

Add the vegetables to the dish and fry them for about 8 minutes or until they start to take on some colour. Next, add the flour and stir well. Then pour in the wine, stock and herbs and season well. Return the lamb shanks to the dish and bring the mixture up to the boil.

Cover with a lid and cook the shanks in the oven for $2\frac{1}{2}$–3 hours (depending on how large they are), after which time the lamb should be falling off the bone. Turn the shanks halfway through the cooking time so that both sides soak up all the flavour and moisture from the cooking liquid.

When the lamb is cooked remove it from the dish, cover it with foil to keep it hot, and set aside. Taste the liquid and adjust the seasoning if necessary and sieve it into a bowl. Remove the bay leaf and thyme stalks from the vegetables left in the sieve, place them in a serving dish and keep warm. If you'd like the liquid to be thicker transfer it to a pan and simmer it on the hob over a medium high heat for about 10 minutes, to reduce it down. Transfer the cooking liquid to a serving jug and serve it with the lamb, vegetables and mashed potato.

# Steak, Camembert and Mushroom Pancakes

Thick, oozing Camembert cheese melting over steak, onion and mushrooms, all wrapped up in a pancake is pretty damn good in my opinion. Perfect with a green salad on the side and a bottle of robust red wine.

**Makes 4 pancakes**

**For the pancakes**
60g plain flour
1 egg
150ml semi-skimmed milk
vegetable oil, for cooking

**For the filling**
2 large, flat mushrooms
olive oil
1 onion, sliced
250g rump or sirloin steak, thickly sliced into strips
100g Camembert, thickly sliced
sea salt and freshly ground black pepper

Preheat the oven to 200°C/ fan 180°C /Gas Mark 6.

To make the batter for the pancakes, sift the flour into a medium mixing bowl and make a well in the centre, then crack the egg into it. Whisk the egg, gradually incorporating the flour until it starts to form a paste and then slowly mix in the milk using a small whisk, so that you get a smooth mixture the consistency of single cream. Leave the batter to stand for 30 minutes.

Once the batter has rested you can start making the filling for the pancakes. Wipe any dirt from the mushrooms (never wash them as they're porous and will absorb water) then slice them. Heat a little olive oil in a non-stick frying pan over a medium heat then add the mushrooms and onion. Sauté them for a couple of minutes, then turn the heat up to high, add the steak and continue sautéing for a few more minutes, stirring regularly with a wooden spoon, until everything is cooked through. Keep warm in the pan, covered with foil, while you make the pancakes.

To make the pancakes brush a little oil onto the bottom of an 18–20cm frying pan using a pastry brush or some kitchen towel. Heat the pan over a high heat so that it's nice and hot and then turn the heat down to medium. Add a ladleful of batter to the pan and swirl it around so that it covers the bottom of the pan. Cook for 1–2 minutes or until the bottom of the pancake starts to turn golden. You can check this by loosening the edges with a palette knife and checking underneath. When the bottom of the pancake is cooked flip it over with the palette knife or by tossing it in the air. The other side won't take as long to cook; only about 30–60 seconds. Place the cooked pancake on a plate with a sheet of greaseproof paper on top. Repeat to make 3 more pancakes, layering them with greaseproof paper as they are cooked.

Put a quarter of the steak mixture in the middle of each pancake with a quarter of the Camembert. Roll the pancakes up and place them on a medium non-stick baking tray and bake them in the oven for about 5 minutes or so, until the cheese starts to melt. Serve straight away.

**Cook's notes**
When you're making these have the mushrooms, onions, steak and Camembert already sliced before your guests arrive and the flour and milk for the pancakes measured out. All you need to do then is whisk up the batter, leave it to rest while you have a drink with your friends and then fry up the filling and whip up the pancakes. Pop them in the oven for 5 minutes and there you have it; dinner in a flash.

# Pear, Fig and Stichelton Salad

Stichelton is a British blue cheese, similar to Stilton, but made from unpasteurised milk instead of pasteurised, as Stilton is. For more information about Stichelton and where you can buy it visit www.stichelton.co.uk. It's quite lovely but Stilton would work just as well as an alternative in this beautiful salad.

**Serves 2 as a main course or 4 as a starter**

4 handfuls of watercress
4 figs, quartered
2 ripe pears, cored and thickly
   sliced (green Williams' pears are
   my favourite)
approximately 200g Stichelton or
   Stilton cheese
extra virgin olive oil
freshly ground black pepper
   (optional)

Divide the watercress between 2 or 4 plates then arrange the figs and pears over. Crumble over the cheese and drizzle over a little olive oil just before serving. Season with black pepper, if liked.

# Roasted Potato Wedges

A huge bowl of thick, chunky, roasted wedges sprinkled with sea salt and served with mayonnaise or a big dollop of soured cream is always a real crowd pleaser.

**Serves 4**

1kg floury potatoes, e.g. King Edward or Maris Piper, cut lengthways into wedges, skin on
olive oil
sea salt

Preheat the oven to 220°C/fan 200°C/gas mark 7.

Bring a large pan of salted water to the boil then add the potato wedges and parboil them for 5 minutes, making sure they don't cook all the way through. Drain the wedges and leave them to dry out on some kitchen paper or a clean tea towel for 5 minutes.

Put the potato wedges onto a baking tray, pour the olive oil over and toss well to cover them. If you want to add any flavourings, do so at this stage (see Cook's notes).

Put the potatoes into the oven and cook them for 40 minutes, or until crisp and golden. Sprinkle them with sea salt before serving.

**Cook's notes**
Parboiling the wedges ensures they're fluffy on the inside and leaving them to dry out before roasting helps them to crisp up perfectly.

You can vary the wedges by sprinkling over different flavourings, such as crushed garlic, finely chopped rosemary or thyme, paprika, cayenne pepper or chilli, or a mixture of some of them, just after you coat the wedges in the olive oil.

# Roasted Vegetables

When vegetables are roasted like this they become incredibly sweet and toe-curlingly good. They're great with a roast dinner but also on the side of simply grilled meat or even on their own as a main dish, especially if you add some cheese toward the end of the cooking time (see Cook's notes). And if you have any leftover they make a great soup; whizzed up with some vegetable stock and a few fresh herbs.

**Serves 4**

1 butternut squash, peeled, deseeded and cut into bite-sized chunks
1 sweet potato, cut into bite-sized chunks
2 onions, cut into bite-sized chunks
2 red or yellow peppers, deseeded and cut into bite-sized chunks
4 carrots, cut into bite-sized chunks
olive oil
sea salt and freshly ground black pepper

Preheat the oven to 200°C/ fan 180°C/gas mark 6.

Place the vegetables in a large roasting tin. Drizzle a little olive oil over the vegetables and then toss to coat them thoroughly, season well.

Roast the vegetables for approximately 45–60 minutes, turning them once during the cooking time, until tender when pierced with a knife.

**Cook's notes**
The temperature in the recipe is the one I would use if I were roasting vegetables in the oven on their own. However, if I were roasting something else, like chicken or beef, at the same time, at a lower temperature I would still cook the vegetables at the same time and then just turn the heat right up, to 230°C/fan 210°C/gas mark 8, once the meat has been removed from the oven and is resting. You can always cover the meat with foil to keep it warm if the vegetables take a little longer than the resting time of the meat.

The list of vegetables is simply a suggestion; feel free to change them depending on what you have in or what you fancy – courgettes, parsnips, aubergines or shallots all work well too. For a change try adding herbs or garlic, either a bulb broken into cloves, skin kept on so that they roast in it and turn beautifully sweet, or crushed and sprinkled over the vegetables for a stronger taste. And if you wanted you could add some cubes of cheese 10 minutes before the end of the cooking time; I like to use fontina or mozzarella.

# Cheese Sauce for Vegetables

Fresh, green vegetables smothered in hot cheese sauce are really good and great on the side of chicken (perhaps a griddled or baked chicken breast) or beef (slices of roast beef or steak).

500ml full fat or semi-skimmed
  milk
40g butter
40g plain flour
75g mature Cheddar cheese, grated
75g Parmesan cheese, grated

Gently heat the milk in a small non-stick pan and keep it warm.

In a separate small non-stick pan melt the butter over a low-medium heat then add the flour, stirring continuously with a wooden spoon until it forms a smooth paste. Cook the paste for 5 minutes, stirring now and then.

Slowly add the milk to the roux, stirring continuously with a wooden spoon to prevent lumps from forming. As the mixture loosens up with the milk change to a whisk and whisk in the rest of the milk. Simmer the sauce until it thickens, whisking regularly, and then stir in the cheese.

Pour the sauce over cooked vegetables such as broccoli, leeks, asparagus or purple sprouting broccoli.

**Cook's note**
The basis of a white sauce, such as the one for this cheese sauce, is a roux, which is a paste made by stirring and cooking butter and flour together. A roux is a very handy thing to know how to make as it can also be added to sauces or gravies to thicken them up.

# Chicken in Lemon and White Wine

I love this simple chicken in its wine-doused creamy sauce. Mashed potato is the perfect partner for soaking it all up. I tend to use the juice of half a lemon, which makes the sauce very lemony, but if you prefer use just a squeeze. You can always use a little at the beginning and add more just before serving if you think it needs it.

**Serves 4**

olive oil
4 free range chicken legs
250ml dry white wine
200ml double cream
a large bunch of flat-leaf parsley, chopped
juice of $\frac{1}{2}$ lemon
sea salt and freshly ground black pepper
mashed potatoes, asparagus, baby carrots or runner beans, to serve

Preheat the oven to 200°C/fan 180°C/gas mark 6.

Heat a little oil in a flameproof casserole dish and fry the chicken over a high heat for 8–10 minutes or until golden on the outside. Add the wine to the dish and allow it to sizzle and reduce for a minute or so then add the cream, half the parsley and a squeeze of lemon juice. Season generously and stir everything together well. Bring the mixture to the boil then put the dish into the oven, uncovered. Cook for 40 minutes, turning the chicken half way through.

After 40 minutes check the chicken is cooked through, when the thickest part of the leg is pierced and the juices run clear, then transfer it to plates. Taste the sauce and add more seasoning or lemon juice if necessary, and stir through the remaining parsley. Pour the sauce over the chicken before serving with the mash and vegetables.

# Blueberry Cheesecakes

These individual cheesecakes are so easy to make and great for a dinner party. Make them well in advance to give them time to chill and firm up in the fridge.

The amount of sugar you'll need in the filling will depend on the type of cream cheese you use and, of course, your own preference, so mix in a little, taste it then add more as you need.

**Makes 4 individual cheesecakes**

**For the base**
75g digestive biscuits
25g butter

**For the filling**
300g full fat cream cheese
icing sugar, to taste
1 teaspoon vanilla extract
a squeeze of lemon juice, to taste
 (optional)

**For the topping**
150g blueberries
60g caster sugar

You can make the cheesecakes in 9cm ramekins or using 9cm metal ring moulds. If you're using ramekins, line them completely with foil, letting it over extend the top so you can easily pull the cheesecakes out.

Place the biscuits in a plastic food bag and crush them with a rolling pin until they form even-sized crumbs. Place the butter in a medium pan and heat it gently until melted. Stir the crumbs into the melted butter. Place the metal rings or ramekins onto serving plates then press a quarter of the biscuit mixture into each. Set aside to cool in the fridge.

Place the cream cheese and vanilla extract in a medium bowl and mix them together until smooth. Add a tablespoon of icing sugar at a time, mixing well, until the filling is sweet enough for your taste. Stir in a squeeze of lemon juice, if liked. Spoon the mixture over the bases in the rings or ramekins and smooth over the tops. Chill in the fridge for at least 4 hours.

While the filling is setting, make the topping. Gently heat the blueberries and sugar together in a small pan, for about 15 minutes, swirling the pan now and again, until the blueberries start to break down and the sugar completely dissolves. Allow the mixture to cool and refrigerate it until you're ready to serve the cheesecakes.

When the cheesecakes are set and you are ready to serve them, if you've used ramekins simply pull the foil away from the sides of each cheesecake and transfer to a plate using a metal fish slice. If you've used metal rings use a blowtorch to heat the moulds a little, to make them easier to slide off or, if you haven't got a blowtorch, wrap a hot cloth around them for a minute. Spoon the blueberry topping over the cheesecakes just before serving.

# Caramelised Orange Puffs

The combination of fresh oranges and sweet caramel is quite delicious and especially nice served sitting on little puff pastry beds.

**Serves 4–6**

flour, for dusting
375g ready-rolled puff pastry
2 oranges, peeled and segmented
100g caster sugar
a knob of butter
60ml hot water from a recently boiled kettle

Preheat the oven to 200°C/ fan 180°C/gas mark 6. Line 2 large baking trays with baking parchment.

Lightly flour a worksurface and place the ready-rolled pastry sheet on it. Using a 7cm round cutter cut out 12 discs of pastry and place them on the baking trays. Bake the puffs in the oven for 10–12 minutes, until they're puffed up and golden then remove them and allow them to cool on a wire rack. These can be made a few hours in advance if desired.

If serving straight away, once cool place the pastry discs onto plates (3 each if you're serving 4 people, 2 each if you have 6 guests) and lay the orange segments over the discs.

Before you start making the caramel have the water ready in a jug next to the hob so that when you're ready to add it you don't need to worry about measuring it out.

Heat a small, heavy-based, non-stick frying pan over a medium high heat then add the sugar to the pan. Shake it so that the sugar is evenly distributed in one layer. After a while it will start to dissolve and turn golden. Shake the pan every now and then so that the sugar dissolves evenly. Never take your eyes off the pan, and be patient; don't be tempted to turn the heat up too high as the caramel can quickly get too hot, which can be alarming, and it will over-cook and take on a bitter, burnt taste. Once the sugar has completely

dissolved and turned a deep, golden, caramel colour, put an oven glove on and take the pan off the heat, then hold it at arms length and add the butter to the pan, taking care as the caramel may splutter. Swirl the pan as the butter melts then add the water to the pan, still holding it at arms length, as it will splutter and steam violently when the water is added. Swirl the pan to mix the water into the caramel and then pour it over the oranges and pastry discs and serve immediately.

**Cook's note**
The caramel may seize a little when you add the water resulting in hard lumps forming. In which case you can either just discard the lumps and pour the rest of the sauce over the orange puffs or return the pan to the heat to melt the lumps.

The caramel sauce is very versatile and delicious over roasted fruits or vanilla ice cream, perhaps with some chopped nuts.

## Making caramel

Making caramel can be a tricky business but I've learned that if you follow a few golden rules (If you'll forgive the pun!) you'll have little trouble with it. It's a great thing to know how to make and it can transform desserts into quite spectacular dishes.

*Golden rule 1:*
*Be careful and never touch or be tempted to taste hot caramel.*
Caramelisation occurs when sugar reaches around 170°C – much higher than boiling water – and it can very quickly get a great deal hotter, so never take your eyes off sugar or caramel that's on the heat. Caramel sticks to everything, including skin, and is scalding hot so will burn you terribly. It will spit and splutter when liquid or butter is added to it so hold it at arms length, wearing an oven glove, if you need to do this and take care.

*Golden rule 2:*
*Be patient.*
You need a medium high heat to make caramel. You don't want to heat the sugar too quickly; it needs to be controlled. I once set off my fire alarm by heating it too quickly and the smoking was quite alarming. Nothing will appear to happen for quite some time but wait and watch; it will get there.

*Golden rule 3:*
*Get the caramel to the right point.*
You need the flavour of the molasses in the sugar to come out to give the special taste of caramel and you need to be confident enough to allow it to reach a deep, golden amber colour for that to happen, so you don't want to take it off the heat too soon – if you do the caramel will be too sweet. Equally, however, it can quickly over-cook and take on a bitter taste. If you're unsure the best thing to do is to take the pan off the heat, check the colour and put it back on if necessary. You could also have some water in the sink ready to plunge the pan into to cool it down if it starts to cook too much. Your nose, as well as your eyes, will tell you when it's reached that wonderful caramel stage.

*Golden rule 4:*
*Heat the sugar evenly.*
Once you've poured the sugar into your pan shake it so that the sugar forms an even layer, and while it's heating shake the pan every now and then so that the sugar dissolves evenly, otherwise you may end up with bits of it cooking quicker and burning before it's all turned to caramel.

*Golden rule 5:*
*Decide before you start if you want hard set or liquid..*
Once your sugar has turned to caramel you can use it as it is, pouring it over nuts as in the recipe on page 186, for example, and it will set hard. Alternatively you can add butter, water or cream to the hot caramel – carefully, see Golden rule #1 – to give you a liquid caramel such as a creamy sauce. Either way make the decision before you start making the caramel; once it's off the heat it will quickly start to cool and harden so you need to have everything to hand.

One final thing: to clean a pan of caramel fill it with water and bring it to the boil, which will melt the caramel.

# Strawberry Chocolate Meringues

I adore meringues; I get great pleasure in breaking into their crisp shells and finding gooey deliciousness inside, and I love how they simply melt on the tongue. Topped with lightly whipped cream and fresh strawberries, and drizzled with warm white chocolate, they make a charming dessert or afternoon treat.

**Makes 6–8 meringues**

**For the meringues**
3 egg whites
165g caster sugar

**For the topping**
250ml double cream, lightly
    whipped
200g strawberries, hulled

**For the white chocolate**
50g white chocolate
2 tablespoons double cream

Preheat the oven to 120°C/fan 100°C/gas mark ¼. Line 2 large baking trays with baking parchment.

Place the egg whites into a large mixing bowl. Whisk the eggs until they form stiff peaks (see Cook's notes for Summer Pavlova, page 43). Next add the sugar one tablespoon at a time, whisking each tablespoon in before adding the next. Once all the sugar has been incorporated the mixture should be firm and glossy.

Spoon the mixture onto the baking parchment on the trays, forming 6 to 8 mounds of meringue, depending on your number of guests. Shape each one nicely – they'll expand a little but pretty much set in the shape you make them – and create a slight dip in the middle of each one to hold the cream once they're cooked and cooled. Bake the meringues for 1¾–2 hours until crisp, then remove them from the oven and leave them to cool.

Spoon some of the whipped double cream into the meringues. Top them with the strawberries, either chopped or left whole as you prefer.

Bring a small pan of water to the boil then put the chocolate and cream into a heatproof bowl and place the bowl over the pan of water, making sure it doesn't touch the water. Stir the chocolate into the cream as it melts and once it's completely melted take it off the heat and drizzle it over the meringues. Serve the meringues straight away or chill in the fridge for a couple of hours.

*Pooh always liked a little something at eleven o'clock in the morning, and he was very glad to see Rabbit getting out the plates and mugs; and when Rabbit said, 'Honey or condensed milk with your bread?' he was so excited that he said 'Both,' and then, so as not to seem greedy, he added, 'But don't bother about the bread please.'*

Winnie the Pooh A. A. Milne

# Pomegranate and Passion Fruit Jellies

Extracting the juice from the fruits was messy and not especially easy, and I was rather disheartened by the end of the exercise to find that even though I'd bought 6 passionfruits and 2 pomegranates, I only had just ~~under~~ under 300ml of juice. It seemed rather little reward for what had been a fair amount of effort. But when I tasted the finished jellies I was so blown away by the intense, explosive fruitiness, captured in soft gelatine, I knew the recipe was a keeper.

Blog entry, March 2009

These small shots of fruity jelly are a great way of ending a meal on a high note. They really are worth the effort.

**Makes 4 small jellies**

2 pomegranates
6 passion fruits
4 leaves of platinum grade gelatine
80g caster sugar

Cut the pomegranates in half and squeeze out as much of the juice as you can into a measuring jug. Then extract the pips that are still surrounded by juice and push them through a sieve over the jug, bursting them with a spoon, to retrieve as much juice as possible. Next cut the passion fruits in half and scoop out the flesh and seeds, again pushing them through a sieve to extract the juice. You should get

somewhere around 300ml juice. Make it up to 500ml with cold water.

Soak the gelatine leaves in water, according to the packet instructions, Gently heat the juice and sugar in a small pan, stirring as the sugar dissolves. Once the sugar has dissolved, stir in the soaked gelatine and stir until it dissolves.

Allow the mixture to cool a little then pour it into 4 small individual moulds – ramekins are the ideal size for these. Put the jellies into the fridge overnight or through the day to allow them to set.

To turn the jellies out, dip the moulds in hot water first to loosen them away from the sides and then invert them onto individual serving plates.

# Rosé Wine and Strawberry Jellies

These jellies are delicate and summery, and a lovely way to end a summer meal with friends. The wine really brings out the aroma of the strawberries making the jellies smell absolutely delicious.

Please be aware that these are alcoholic jellies; the alcohol is not cooked off so do warn your guests, drivers in particular, and offer a non-alcoholic alternative if necessary.

**Serves 4**

5 leaves of platinum grade gelatine
500ml rosé wine
150g caster sugar
200g strawberries, hulled and
  quartered
double cream, to serve (optional)

Soak the gelatine leaves in water, according to the packet instructions.

Gently heat the wine, 200ml of water and sugar in a medium pan, stirring occasionally until the sugar dissolves. Don't allow the mixture to boil. Once the sugar has dissolved add the gelatine to the mixture and stir it until it dissolves.

Allow the mixture to cool a little before pouring it into 4 serving glasses. Add the strawberries to each glass where they will sit at the top of the jelly. When the mixture has cooled put the glasses into the fridge overnight or through the day to allow the jellies to set.

If you like, you can very lightly whip a little double cream and top each glass with about 2–3cm of cream before serving.

# Honey Peaches

These honey-coated peaches are lovely served with lightly whipped cream, mascarpone or vanilla ice cream.

**Serves 4**

4 ripe peaches, halved and stoned
a knob of butter
3 tablespoons clear honey

Put the peaches skin side down in a bowl of boiling water for about 1 minute to loosen the skins so that you can carefully peel them.

Heat the butter in a medium non-stick frying plan until it melts and then add the peaches and the honey. Cook over a low medium heat for about 6–8 minutes, spooning the honey and butter mixture over the peaches as they cook, until the liquid turns syrupy. Serve the peaches with a little of the syrup poured over.

# The Cheeseboard

If you truly love your friends and family give them cheese to round off the meal. Presenting a board holding two or three large wedges of good cheeses, along with crusty bread and a bottle of port, may just be the culinary equivalent of those sacred gifts of gold, frankincense and myrrh. If you like you can dress the cheeseboard up a little with grapes, figs, or quarters of apples or pears, but the stars of this show are the cheeses so make sure they're good ones.

Having spent years buying only supermarket cheeses, walking into Neal's Yard Dairy at Borough Market for the first time was an eye-opening, and taste bud-awakening, experience. The shop groans under the weight of shelves and shelves of huge wheels of cheeses – all British, all different – and you're invited to try any you like. The choice is quite overwhelming so it's good to have the cheesemongers on hand to give recommendations.

You'll hear cooks and food lovers, myself included, talk a lot about using good quality ingredients, but they can be more expensive so it's good to know when it's worth spending a little bit more and when it doesn't make so much difference, so that you can spend a little extra where it matters the most. And when it comes to cheeses, it matters. Factory produced and hand-made cheeses are a world apart and once you've tasted really good, proper cheese you'll feel hard-done by when you eat most supermarket plastic wrapped ones.

I don't profess to be a cheese connoisseur – far from it – but I've learned a few basics to enable me to produce and enjoy a good cheeseboard. You may well already know these points but in case, like me a few years back, you feel a little daunted when it comes to cheese, let me share them with you:

• When buying cheese from a cheese shop or cheese counter of a supermarket ask to try the cheeses – a good cheesemonger will offer anyway. Let him or her guide you and don't feel shy or embarrassed about asking questions and for recommendations. And don't feel pressured into buying a particular cheese; only buy what you really like the taste of.

• Think simplicity and quality. You'll be much better off – as will your guests – if you buy two really good cheeses rather than five cheaper ones. You could even buy just one real star cheese such as a Colston Bassett Stilton and let it steal the show; especially good at Christmas.

• For a classic board choose one soft, one hard and one blue cheese, and choose differing strengths rather than all mild or all strong. You can't go far wrong with Brie, Cheddar and Stilton.

• Cheese should ideally be stored in a cool, slightly damp place such as a cellar, as what they need is humidity rather than a cold temperature. The fridge is really one of the worst places you can store cheese as it can dry it out but since few of us have our own cellar these days the best thing to do is to wrap cheese in waxed paper or baking parchment – never clingfilm – and put it in the salad drawer of the fridge, preferably with some salad vegetables to create some humidity.

• Take the cheeses out of the fridge 1–2 hours before serving them. This allows them to warm up which brings their flavours back to life, as the cold kills their flavour.

• Arrange the cheeses on a board so that they're not touching each other and there is enough space between them to easily cut them. A wooden board is traditional and the one I favour but of course you can use any board you like.

• Use separate knives for each cheese to avoid cross-contaminating them and mixing up the flavours.

• I sometimes offer crusty bread with my cheeseboard but also love to serve a good selection of biscuits such as water biscuits, digestives and charcoal biscuits. I don't usually eat them with butter but it is nice to offer salted butter to guests.

• And finally, I always enjoy my cheese with a glass of good port – I love to serve a nice late bottled vintage port and particularly like those with rich, fruity and chocolaty back-notes.

**Three of my favourites...**

**Roquefort**. I love this sharp, creamy and crumbly blue cheese, which is ripened in the caves of Mount Combalou in the Roquefort-sur-Soulzon region of France. It makes a delicious alternative to Stilton on your cheeseboard.

**Comté** is a hard cheese made from the milk of the cows that graze in the mountains of eastern France close to the Swiss border. It has a fairly rich flavour, slightly sweet and nutty, that is quite lovely.

**Wensleydale** is a delicious cheese made in the Yorkshire Dales, which makes a nice change from Cheddar. It has a creamy, fairly strong and distinct flavour.

Autumn days, when
the grass is jewelled,
And the silk inside
a chestnut shell,
Jet planes meeting in
the air to be refuelled,
All these things I love
so well.

Estelle White, *Autumn Days*

# rain on glass

Autumn is a wonderful time of year, full of visual and culinary opulence. As much as I love summer, I welcome the change autumn brings and the fresher air after long, hot, sultry days. I look forward to wrapping up in jumpers, curling up on the sofa when it's dark and cold outside, watching fireworks light up the sky on Bonfire Night, kicking the red and gold leaves and, of course, enjoying the food.

Of all the seasons this is surely the most exciting and inspiring for the cook. The earth gives generously in the autumn, leaving us spoilt for choice. There's an abundance of fruit, vegetables and nuts to choose from – apples and pears, pumpkins and squashes, mushrooms, blackberries, chestnuts – and robust meats, such as pork, venison, autumn lamb and game birds. Cooking slows down and meals become heartier and more homely. My kitchen never seems more welcoming than at this time of year.

I have fond memories of autumn from my childhood. My sister and I would take the long walk to school each morning with Mum, passing through a small stretch of woodland on the way where we would gather fallen leaves for art work and sweet mahogany chestnuts in their prickly shells to take home and roast. My school celebrated the Harvest Festival and Mum would give my sister and me tins of food and vegetables to put into the boxes at the school that were to be distributed to the elderly. The next event on the calendar was Halloween, for which Mum would bake biscuits and we'd play apple bobbing whilst dressed up as witches in home-made costumes with painted faces. On Bonfire Night, less than a week later, we would eat baked potatoes with melting butter and sausages in long rolls with caramelised onions and ketchup before going into the garden to write our names in the smoky night air with sparklers.

These are the memories I take with me into the kitchen in the autumn months when I'm baking crumbles, bubbling and oozing their hot fruit juices, slowly frying sticky sausages, chopping vegetables for rich casseroles, and checking soups for seasoning as they simmer on the hob, steaming up the windows. They're the memories that make me smile and seem to somehow infuse my cooking with a little of the magic of times gone by.

# Sausage and Sweet Potato Mash

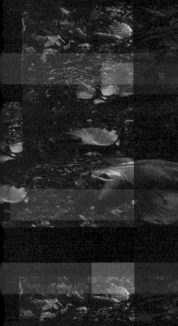

Serve in a bowl and curl up
on the sofa while the autumn
leaves dance in the wind outside.

Blog entry, September 2006

As sad as it is to say goodbye to
summer there's a sweetness
in saying 'hello' to a new season
and a new chapter.

Blog entry, September 2009

I love the back-to-school feeling I still get when the year moves on into September and I see the first of the leaves turning on the trees. But instead of new pencils and books I now buy knee-length boots and long, woolly scarves.

Along with the back-to-school feeling come the thoughts of more robust, comforting meals such as this one, which was the first thing I ever posted on my blog. I called that first post 'Autumn in a Bowl' and suggested this was the perfect dish to welcome in autumn. I still feel the same about it.

**Serves 4**

olive oil
8 good quality sausages
1 large onion, halved and sliced
1 tablespoon plain flour
150ml marsala
150ml beef stock
$\frac{1}{2}$ teaspoon dried oregano
sea salt and freshly ground black
    pepper

**For the sweet potato mash**
4 sweet potatoes, peeled and cut
    into large cubes
a generous knob of butter

Heat a little olive oil in a large, non-stick frying pan then add the sausages and fry them over a low heat for about 20 minutes, until they're sticky and golden brown but not yet cooked through.

Push the sausages to the side of the pan then add the onion and continue to cook over a low heat for about 20 minutes, until the onion turns soft and golden and the sausages are cooked through.

Meanwhile, for the sweet potato mash, put the potatoes in a large pan of salted water, bring to the boil then cook for 15–20 minutes or until tender.

Once the onion is cooked increase the heat and add the flour to the pan, stirring it in. Add the marsala and let it sizzle away before adding the beef stock and oregano. Turn the heat down to medium and gently simmer the gravy until it thickens up. Season to taste.

Drain the potatoes then mash them with the butter and a good sprinkling of salt.

Serve the sausages with a good helping of the mash and some of the gravy.

# English Cheddar Soup

I never thought I'd find a soup as comforting as chicken soup but on a cold, grey day this really hits the spot. The Cheddar is distinctive, but not overpowering, and so you get a lovely tang at the back of your throat and yet the soup is creamy, comforting and soothing. Although it's perfect comfort food, it's also sophisticated enough to hold its own as a dinner party starter.

**Serves 6**

25g butter
1 large shallot, diced
2 large potatoes, diced
1 litre chicken stock
300g good quality extra mature
    English Cheddar cheese, grated
    (see Cook's notes)
100ml double cream (optional)
sea salt and white pepper (see
    Cook's notes)
chopped chives, to garnish
    (optional)
thick crusty bread, to serve

Melt the butter in a large pan and fry the shallot gently for a few minutes until it starts to soften. Add the potatoes and stock to the pan, bring to a boil and simmer until the potatoes are cooked through. Blend the soup, in the pan using a hand blender, until smooth.

Turn the heat down to medium low and then add the cheese. Keep the soup on the heat and stir for a few minutes, stirring regularly, until it thickens and the cheese has completely melted into it. Don't allow it to boil and watch it carefully as it will boil over like milk if left.

Take the soup off the heat, season it to taste and add the cream, if using. Blend it once more to make it nice and smooth. Add a little water if the soup is too thick for your liking. If you like you can garnish the soup with chopped chives for a fleck of colour and a mild onion flavour. Serve the soup with thick, crusty bread for dipping and coating.

**Cook's notes**
English Cheddar cheese originates from the village that lends it its name – Cheddar in Somerset, and it dates back to at least 1170. It has a firm, slightly crumbly texture and can have a slightly sharp tang to it. When buying it look out for West Country Farmhouse Cheddar – the certification of the real thing – on the label and choose Somerset Cheddar where possible. It's particularly important that you buy very good quality Cheddar for this recipe: this soup is all about the cheese and the better the quality the better the taste; to be honest there's no point in making it with anything less than the best. And you do need strong extra mature Cheddar for this soup; with anything milder the flavour won't permeate the soup enough.

The choice of white pepper is purely for aesthetics – as this is a white soup I don't really want it specked with black – but if you're not concerned by this then by all means uses black pepper.

# Creamy Sausage Pasta

This hearty dish is fabulous on a wet and windy day. The creamy sauce is flavoured by the sausages and onions and everything comes together in one rib-sticking pasta dish.

**Serves 4–6**

olive oil
8 good quality pork sausages, each cut into 6 pieces
1 large onion, halved and sliced
200ml double cream
200ml beef stock
2 sprigs thyme
300g dried pasta shapes, e.g. farfalle or fusilli
sea salt and freshly ground black pepper

Heat a little olive oil in a large frying pan and brown the sausage pieces. When they're almost, but not quite, cooked through remove them from the pan. Next add the onion to the same pan which should now have some lovely, sticky brown bits left from the sausages, and fry them gently for 15 minutes, until they are softened and lightly golden. Then turn the heat up high and cook the onions for a few minutes more until they turn darker golden brown.

Return the sausages to the pan along with the cream, beef stock and thyme. Bring the cream and stock to the boil and season it with salt and black pepper, then simmer it until the sausages are cooked through and the sauce thickens, which will take about 20–25 minutes.

While the sauce is simmering bring a large pan of salted water to the boil then add the pasta. Bring the water back up to the boil and cook the pasta according to the pack instructions, until *al dente* – soft on the outside but still a little firm in the middle. Drain the pasta.

Check the seasoning in the sauce then add the pasta to it and mix it all together well before serving.

# Pot Roast Chicken

*Monday Evening.*

This is one of those wonderful one-pot dishes that does all the work for you as it cooks away in the oven, creating homely smells, succulent chicken and a golden broth, leaving you to pour another cup of tea and put your feet up for a while as the rain pitter-patters against the window pane. After roast chicken it's my favourite chicken dish; I simply love curling up with a small bowlful of the glorious broth with some of the vegetables and chicken, especially when I'm feeling under the weather.

Do feel free to pick and choose what vegetables and herbs you put in with the chicken – or just use whatever you have in – and for some more bulk to the meal add potatoes to the pot, peeled and cut into chunks.

**Serves 4**

1 free-range chicken, preferably
   organic, approximately 1.8kg
1 large onion, halved and finely
   sliced
8 Chantenay or baby carrots
2 leeks, sliced
2 bay leaves
a few sprigs of rosemary and/or
   thyme
a handful of flat-leaf parsley
sea salt and freshly ground black
   pepper

Preheat the oven to 200°C/ fan 180°C/gas mark 6.

Put the chicken, vegetables, herbs and 500ml cold water into a large casserole dish with a lid and season everything well. Put on the lid and then bake the chicken for 1 hour then remove the lid to allow the chicken to brown. Bake it for a further 30 minutes or until the chicken is cooked through and the juices run clear.

Remove the chicken from the dish, place it on a plate and carve slices of breast and leg meat.

To serve, place some of the vegetables and broth into four bowls along with some slices of the chicken.

**Cook's note**
If you like lots of broth add 500ml chicken stock to the pot along with the cold water before baking.

# Autumnal Chicken

The colours of autumn weave their way into everything: the trees, the new-season's fashions, and our meals. This dish, in particular, puts me in mind of a landscape painter's palette with its golden chicken, burnt-red sweet potato and amber butternut squash. And the fresh green of the parsley reminds me of the leaves changing on the tree, the deep green turning through a spectrum of colours until the leaf flutters to the ground where it finally turns crisp and brown.

**Serves 4**

olive oil
4 chicken legs
1 butternut squash, cut into bite-sized pieces
1 sweet potato, cut into bite-sized pieces
1–2 garlic cloves, crushed
250ml dry white wine
400g can chickpeas
a handful of flat-leaf parsley, chopped
sea salt and freshly ground black pepper

Preheat the oven to 200°C/ fan 180°C/gas mark 6.

Drizzle a little olive oil into a large, non-stick frying pan then brown the chicken in it over a high heat.

Put the chicken legs into a roasting tin along with the butternut squash and sweet potato. Sprinkle over the garlic then season everything with salt and pepper and drizzle over some olive oil. Pour over the white wine then cover the tin with foil and roast it for 30 minutes.

Remove the foil and add the chickpeas to the tin. Give everything a stir and return the tin to the oven for a further 20–30 minutes, until the chicken is cooked through and its juices run clear.

Before serving sprinkle over the chopped parsley and serve with the juices from the pan.

# Tomato and Pasta Soup with Soured Cream

I first heard about this soup many years ago from my friend Viv, who used to make a version of it for lunch when she was working from home, and she shared it with me for when I worked from home. It's such a great storecupboard standby and especially useful if you suddenly find yourself with people to feed. You can vary the base recipe in lots of ways: use different herbs, add garlic or chilli for a kick, fry bacon or chorizo with the onions before adding the tomatoes and stock, or add other vegetables for a more substantial meal.

**Serves 4**

olive oil
1 onion, finely chopped
1–2 sprigs thyme
400g can chopped tomatoes
1 litre vegetable stock
200g small pasta shapes, e.g. conchigliette
sea salt and freshly ground black pepper
soured cream, to garnish

Heat a little olive oil in a large saucepan and fry the onion for about 5 minutes until softened.

Add the leaves from the sprigs of thyme, the chopped tomatoes and vegetable stock. Season well, stir everything together, and bring it to the boil. Add the pasta and simmer the soup for approximately 10 minutes until the pasta is *al dente*.

Once the pasta is cooked, check the seasoning and adjust if necessary, then take the soup off the heat. To serve, ladle it into bowls, add a large dollop of soured cream and eat straight away.

# Baked Sweet Potato

## Solitary food

When I'm feeling peckish and the kitchen is calling I make a favourite snack. Sometimes it's a glass of cold milk and a digestive biscuit or perhaps a chocolate HobNob; sometimes crisp toast slathered with butter and a thin spread of sticky, salty Marmite; sometimes crusty bread and ripe cheese. Then there are the occasions when I want something hot, with a little more sustenance and, although I don't really want to cook a full meal just for myself, a snack just isn't going to be enough. Here are some of my trusty meals for one, for those times.

On those days when it's damp and grey with that fine, drizzly rain in the air, leaving you feeling like a cloud has descended from the skies that just won't disperse, comfort food of the highest order is needed. Soup, mashed potato or cake are all good candidates but something you perhaps may not have thought of is a sweet potato, baked in its skin then mashed with sea salt, freshly ground black pepper and butter. It's wonderfully sweet and fills your tummy with warmth, and the colour of its deep orange flesh is so cheering. An alternative way of serving this is to peel off the skin and mash up the flesh with butter and seasoning, turning it into a great side dish for two people.

1 sweet potato, scrubbed
a large dollop of soured cream
sea salt and freshly ground black
  pepper

Preheat the oven to 200°C/
fan 180°C/gas mark 6.

Place the potato on a baking tray and bake it for 45–60 minutes, or until it gives when you squeeze it and feels fairly soft inside – the cooking time will depend on the size of the potato.

Break it open, mash the insides up with a fork, sprinkle over some sea salt and freshly ground black pepper then spoon over a generous helping of soured cream and dive in.

## Eggy Bread

Mum used to make me this when I was a child... and a teenager... and an adult. You can never grow out of it as far as I'm concerned. Although the proper name is French Toast I much prefer Eggy Bread – it is what it is!

**Serves 1**

1 egg
1 slice of bread, any type will do
a knob of butter

Beat the egg in a shallow dish. Place the slice of bread in the dish to soak up all the egg, on both sides.

Melt the butter in a medium non-stick frying pan over a medium heat. Fry the bread for 2–3 minutes on each side until it is light golden brown.

**Cook's note**
It's common to cook or serve Eggy Bread with sweet things – cinnamon, fruit or sugar – but I much prefer it with savoury flavours. I like it with a smear of Marmite, plain with a sprinkling of salt and pepper or, in a complete lack of sophistication, with a squirt of tomato ketchup. It's great on its own or with bacon on top: especially when you cook it together with the Eggy Bread in the same pan, as the bread soaks up the bacon fat. Terribly naughty, I know, but oh so good!

# Spaghetti with Butter and Parmesan Cheese

This is perfect solitary food, ideal for when you can't really be bothered to cook but you want something hot and filling, and to feel like you've had a proper meal. The spaghetti coated in melted butter and Parmesan cheese is soul soothing; proof on a plate that the simplest of meals are often the best.

**Serves 1**

100g dried spaghetti
a large knob of butter
salt and freshly grated black
    pepper (optional)
grated Parmesan cheese, to serve

Bring a large pan of salted water to the boil then add the pasta. Bring the water back up to the boil and cook the pasta according to the pack instructions, until *al dente* – soft on the outside but still a little firm in the middle. Drain the pasta.

Pile the pasta onto a plate then coat it with the butter and season with pepper, if liked. Finally, grate over lashings and lashings of Parmesan cheese and devour.

# Brie and Bacon Sandwich

This is another snack that my Mum used to make for me – aren't they the best types? With all that oozing cheese over thick, salty bacon sandwiched between thick crusty bread it's hard to beat.

knob of butter
2 slices crusty bread
2 thick rashers back bacon
2 thick slices Brie

Preheat the grill to high.

Spread the butter over the slices of bread. Fry the bacon in a medium non-stick frying pan until it is lightly cooked. Place it on one of the slices of buttered bread. Lay the Brie over the bacon and then pop the bacon and cheese topped bread under the hot grill. When the Brie has melted top with the other slice of bread, cut it in half and enjoy!

# Pear, Blackberry and Chocolate Tart

This autumnal tart is darkly seductive with its red wine, luscious blackberries and curls of chocolate. Serve it on dusky evenings with the curtains drawn and the lights down low.

If you don't feel like making the pastry just buy a sheet of ready-rolled instead.

**For the shortcrust pastry**
200g plain flour
100g cold butter, cubed
flour, for dusting

**For the filling**
1 vanilla pod
150g caster sugar
400ml red wine
3 firm pears, peeled, cored and cut into eighths, lengthways
150g blackberries
1 tablespoon caster sugar
1 egg, beaten
20g 70% cocoa solids dark chocolate, grated
vanilla ice cream, to serve

To make the pastry, place the flour and butter in a medium mixing bowl or the bowl of a food mixer. Rub the butter into the flour using your fingertips, or use the food mixer, until it resembles breadcrumbs. Add 2–3 tablespoons of cold water to bring it together to form a soft ball of dough with your hands. Place the dough in a plastic food bag and chill it in the fridge for 30 minutes.

Meanwhile, split the vanilla pod lengthways using a sharp knife then run the back of the knife along the middle of each half to remove the seeds. Put the pod and seeds into a small pan along with the sugar and red wine. Bring it up to a simmer, stirring to help dissolve the sugar. Add the pear pieces and poach them, by gently simmering them, for 15 minutes, then allow them to cool in the poaching liquid.

Preheat the oven to 180°C/ fan 160°C/gas mark 4. Line a baking tray with baking parchment.

Dust a worksurface with flour and roll the pastry out into an oblong shape then put it onto the lined baking tray – it's much easier to assemble the tart on a tray than on the worksurface and then try to transfer it.

Remove the pears from the poaching liquid with a slotted spoon (keep the liquid in the pan) and lay them over the pastry. Scatter the blackberries over the tart and then sprinkle the caster sugar over them. Bring the edges of the pastry up over the fruit to form a rustic-style edge then brush the beaten egg over the edges of the pastry to glaze it. Bake the tart for about 35 minutes, until the pastry is lightly golden and cooked through.

Bring the poaching liquid left in the pan up to the boil and then rapidly simmer it to reduce it right down until it's thick and syrupy, and then drizzle it over the tart. Allow the tart to cool a little and then generously grate over the dark chocolate.

Serve the tart warm or cold, with vanilla ice cream.

# Pot Roast Pheasants with Chestnuts and Mushrooms

As the nights start to draw in and I'm lighting candles and turning on the heating for the first time in months I start thinking about the game season. The robust, strong flavour of game meats and birds is just right for autumn, especially when teamed with sweet chestnuts and earthy mushrooms. This dish is particularly autumnal and great for a cosy evening at home.

**Serves 4**

olive oil
2 oven-ready pheasants
1 onion, diced
250g mushrooms, wiped clean and left whole, or roughly chopped if very large
1 tablespoon plain flour
200ml chicken stock
2 sprigs of thyme
a handful of flat-leaf parsley, roughly chopped
250g shelled, cooked chestnuts (pre-roasted, canned or vacuum packed)
sea salt and freshly ground black pepper
seasonal vegetables and potatoes, to serve

Preheat the oven to 170°C/ fan 150°C/gas mark 3.

Heat a little olive oil in a flameproof casserole dish over a high heat then add the pheasants and brown them all over. Remove them from the dish once browned and reduce the heat down to medium.

Add the onion to the dish and sauté it for a minute or so then add the mushrooms. Cook the vegetables for about 5 minutes. Stir in the flour and gradually add the stock, stirring continuously with a wooden spoon. Add the herbs to the dish and season well.

Bring the stock up to a simmer and return the pheasants to the dish. Put on a lid and pop the dish into the oven and cook the pheasants for 40 minutes. After this time add the chestnuts and cook the pheasants for about another 20 minutes or until cooked through. To check that the pheasants are cooked, pull on the legs to check that they have some give in them and can easily be pulled away from the body, and pierce the thigh with a skewer to make sure the juices run clear. The cooking time will depend on the size of the pheasants but average-sized ones should take about 1 hour.

Remove the pheasants from the dish. Spoon off any excess fat from the delicious cooking liquid and either serve it as it is or if you prefer it thicker, boil it on the hob to reduce it down. Serve the pheasant with the sauce and seasonal vegetables and potatoes.

# Roasted Pumpkin and Sweet Potato with Feta Cheese

Feta cheese is great for crumbling over salads or roasted vegetables and it keeps well in the fridge for ages until you open it, so it's great to keep as a standby. I often have a packet in the fridge ready to turn a mediocre midweek meal into something really quite lovely. I like to serve this as a main course but it is also great as a side dish with pork chops.

**Serves 2 as a main course or 4 as a side dish**

1kg pumpkin, cut into bite-sized chunks
1 sweet potato, cut into bite-sized chunks
olive oil
100–200g feta cheese
sea salt and freshly ground black pepper

Preheat the oven to 200°C/ fan 180°C/gas mark 6.

Put the vegetables into a roasting tray and drizzle over some olive oil then sprinkle over some black pepper and sea salt.

Roast the vegetables for 35–45 minutes (depending on the size of the pieces), until they are golden on the outside and soft in the middle. Turn them half way through the cooking time so that they cook evenly.

You can either crumble over the feta cheese once the vegetables are cooked and serve them straight away, or you can crumble over the cheese about 5 minutes before the end of the cooking time to melt it a little.

One of the highlights of Halloween was the iced biscuits Mum used to make for us and the children in the neighbourhood who would call on their rounds of trick or treat. She used to make up little bowls of different coloured icing and hand ice pumpkins, witches, ghosts, black cats, and all sorts of other spooky things. My sister and I used to get to ice our very own biscuits and then lick off the icing we'd painstakingly put on.

# Halloween biscuits

Iced biscuits are so much fun to make and of course they don't have to be Halloween themed – you could make Easter biscuits with coloured flowers or bunnies, Valentines biscuits or Christmas biscuits – the possibilities are endless. For the Halloween biscuits I use a round biscuit cutter but you can have lots of fun with different shaped cutters.

**Makes approximately 15 biscuits**

**For the biscuits**
100g unsalted butter, softened
100g caster sugar
1 large egg, beaten
250g plain flour
flour, for dusting

**For the icing**
150g icing sugar
food colourings of your choice

Preheat the oven to 180°C/ fan 160°C/gas mark 4. Line a baking tray with baking parchment.

Place the butter and sugar in a medium mixing bowl or the bowl of a food mixer and cream them together until light and fluffy. Gradually add the beaten egg to the butter and sugar. Finally, mix in the flour then bring the mixture together with your hands to form a dough. The dough can be used straight away but is best placed in a plastic food bag and chilled in the fridge for at least 30 minutes before you use it.

The dough will be fairly sticky so you'll need to roll it out on a floured worksurface and sprinkle over more flour as needed. Roll the dough out until it's about 5mm thick then cut out shapes using a biscuit cutter and place the shapes on the lined tray. You may need to cook them in batches.

Bake the biscuits for about 10 minutes, but do keep an eye on them, as they may need a few minutes less or a little longer depending on your oven. The biscuits should be lightly golden when cooked. When they are cooked put them onto a wire rack to cool.

Once the biscuits have cooled you can ice them. To make the icing, place the icing sugar in a medium mixing bowl and add a few tablespoons of cold water, mixing well to form a paste. You want the paste to be fairly thick so that it won't run off the biscuits when you ice them. Put the icing into separate small bowls and add a few drops of different food colouring to each bowl. Ice the biscuits either using an icing bag with a writing nozzle or a spoon and knife to spread the icing out on the biscuits.

# Baked Pumpkins

Ever since I saw Hugh Fearnley-Whittingstall fill small pumpkins with cream and Gruyère cheese on an episode of River Cottage I've thought this is the perfect autumnal treat. It's a great way of cooking small pumpkins and squashes and I love that they become individual soup bowls, ready to be served straight from the oven.

This recipe is my adaption of Hugh's. I fill the pumpkins with a combination of cream and chicken stock, and I add sage and nutmeg for herby warmth. The volume of chicken stock and cream required will vary according to the size of the pumpkin or squash, so the quantities given below are rough approximations.

Try varying the recipe yourself, as I have, using different cheeses, herbs or spices.

**Serves 1 as a main course**

1 small pumpkin or squash,
    e.g. baby bear or acorn
approximately 100ml chicken stock
approximately 100ml double cream
1 sage leaf
a handful of grated Parmesan
    cheese
1 whole nutmeg
sea salt and freshly ground black
    pepper

Preheat the oven to 190°C/
fan 170°C/gas mark 5.

Slice the top off the pumpkin or squash and set it aside. Scoop out the seeds and fibre from the inside of the pumpkin and discard.

Place the pumpkin or squash on a baking tray and fill it one-third full with chicken stock and one-third full with double cream, so that the liquid comes two-thirds up inside the pumpkin. Mix it together well then pop in the sage leaf, and top the liquid with grated Parmesan. Finally grate over a little nutmeg, season, and pop the top of the pumpkin back on to form a lid.

Bake the pumpkin or squash, for approximately 40–60 minutes, until soft. Check on it during the cooking time to ensure it doesn't collapse through over-cooking.

# Sausage Baguettes with Caramelised Onions

The sight and smell of sausages slowly frying, turning bronze and sticky in the pan, to be fit snugly into long crusty rolls on a bed of caramelised onions, is quite wonderful, especially on Bonfire Night.

Cook the onions on the smallest ring on your hob, on the lowest heat. They'll take about 40 minutes but cooking them slowly like this will allow them the time they need for their natural sugars to caramelise. They're well worth the wait.

**Serves 4**

a knob of butter
olive oil
3–4 onions, halved and sliced
8 pork sausages
butter, for spreading
4 long crusty rolls
tomato ketchup or Tomato relish
    (see recipe on page 68), to serve

Put the butter into a medium pan or small non-stick frying pan along with a little olive oil and melt it over a low heat. Add the onions and cook them gently, stirring occasionally, for about 40 minutes so that they slowly turn soft and golden. At the end of the cooking time turn the heat up to brown the onions.

While the onions are cooking heat a large non-stick frying pan over a low-medium heat, drizzle in the remaining olive oil and add the sausages. Cook them slowly until they're browned and cooked through.

Split and butter the rolls, then divide the onions equally among them and add 2 sausages to each roll. Top with ketchup or Tomato relish, to serve.

# Baked Potatoes

How wonderful the simple baked potato is! Crispy skin broken open to reveal a piping hot inside, ready to be mashed with golden butter and sprinkled with sea salt; this is winter comfort food at its best, perfect for warming you up Bonfire Night.

After simple butter and sea salt my favourite filling is cheese and baked beans, but there are countless choices. I always think classic Bolognese (see recipe on page 161) is particularly good for Bonfire Night.

**Serves 1**

1 large floury baking potato, scrubbed
knob of butter
sea salt

Preheat the oven to 210°C/ fan 190°C/gas mark 6.

Prick the potato all over with a fork. Put it directly onto the oven bars and bake it for between 1 hour and 1 hour 20 minutes – the time will depend on the size and type of potato – until it gives a little when squeezed.

Cut a large cross in the top of the potato and gently squeeze the sides to open it up – using a tea towel so you don't burn your fingers! Mash the insides with a fork and then add the butter and a sprinkling of sea salt.

# Toffee Apples

Delicious autumnal apples coated in sweet toffee make the perfect Bonfire Night treat. Be very careful when making them and follow the same rules for making caramel, on page 111.

**Serves 4**

4 eating apples, e.g. Braeburn, Granny Smith or Royal Gala
100g golden caster sugar
100g light brown sugar
1 teaspoon malt vinegar
25g butter
4 wooden skewers

Push the skewers into the apples through their centres, making sure they're well secured. Set them aside.

Line a baking tray with baking parchment ready for you to put the toffee-coated apples on.

Put the sugar and 100ml water into a medium heavy-based pan and gently heat it until the sugar dissolves. Next, bring the mixture up to the boil and then add the vinegar and butter, swirling the pan as the butter melts to combine it into the mixture. Gently boil the mixture for about 15 minutes, until it turns dark and reaches the 'soft crack' temperature on a sugar thermometer. If you don't have a sugar thermometer drop a little of the mixture into a glass full of cold water and if it sets and turns brittle it's ready. If it's still a little soft boil the mixture for a little longer.

When the mixture is ready carefully dip the apples into the pan, swirling them around in the mixture to cover them well with it. Put them onto the baking parchment-lined baking tray to set and cool, which will take about 10 minutes.

### Rainy days

I love the rain. I find it therapeutic, whether I'm snuggled up indoors listening to it pitter patter down, on a bus watching it make patterns on the cold glass in the windows, or peering out from under a colourful umbrella and feeling the raindrops hit the palm of my open hand. I love the summer rain, that showers the garden leaving everything refreshed and the flowers blooming even brighter, and I love the winter rain, cold and driving, making you feel warm and snug when you're sheltered and dry inside.

Even on those evenings when I'm walking home from work and it's falling so hard it's bouncing back up off the pavement, and I shield myself against it under my umbrella as it soaks my shoulders, my legs, my face, and I'm cold and longing for the moment when I can get back home and shut the door against it...

...still, I love the rain.

On rainy days I like to...
ponder over a jigsaw puzzle...
...curl up by the window with a
good book...
...sketch and paint...
...watch a favourite film...

...make fairy cakes...

# Fairy Cakes

Making fairy cakes is a great rainy day activity for children young and old. When the rain is pouring down and there's nowhere to go and nothing to do it's a great way to pass an hour or so, and turning flour, sugar, butter and eggs into gorgeous little cakes is so very rewarding.

The fairy cakes of my childhood were topped with glacé icing and whilst I have a nostalgic fondness for that I now prefer them with lashings of sweet, girlie buttercream.

## Makes 12

**For the fairy cakes**
125g butter, softened
125g caster sugar
$\frac{1}{2}$ teaspoon vanilla extract
2 eggs
125g self-raising flour, sifted
1 tablespoon milk

**For the buttercream icing**
250g icing sugar
100g butter, softened
food colourings of your choice

Preheat the oven to 200°C/ fan 180°C/gas mark 6.

Place the butter and sugar in a medium mixing bowl or the bowl of a food mixer and cream them together until light and fluffy. Beat in the vanilla extract and then the eggs, one at a time, adding a tablespoon of the flour with each to help prevent the mixture from curdling. Fold in the remaining flour until completely combined, don't beat it in. Mix in approximately 1 tablespoon of milk so that the mixture is of a dropping consistency.

Line a 12 hole patty tin with paper cake cases and then spoon the mixture evenly into them. Bake the cakes for about 12–15 minutes, until lightly golden and springy to the touch. If your oven cooks unevenly, as many do, turn the cake tray around halfway through the cooking time. Once cooked, transfer the cakes to a wire rack to cool

To make the buttercream icing, place the icing sugar and butter in a medium mixing bowl or the bowl of a food mixer and cream them together until light, fluffy and very pale, almost white. Divide the icing among little bowls and add a few drops of different coloured food colouring to each, and mix it in well. Top the cakes with the icing.

**Cook's note**
If you prefer to top your fairy cakes with the glace icing simply add a little hot water to icing sugar to make a smooth, thick icing, which you can then add colouring to.

# wood smoke and roasts

Winter weekends are made for roast dinners, hearty dishes and long, slow cooking; the kind of food that welcomes you home after a long working week and warms you up from the inside out. When you don't have to work at the weekend you can afford a little more time to enjoy a leisurely cooked breakfast, to prepare and gently simmer a Bolognese sauce or to slowly roast a shoulder of lamb throughout the afternoon. It's this pottering, chopping, simmering and slowing of pace that I love at the weekend. Saturday morning is one of my favourite times, when I have the whole weekend stretched out ahead of me and I can flick through cookery books, turn on my laptop and catch up online, sip tea and ponder what I fancy cooking.

In the winter months the traditional Sunday roast really comes into its own, whether it be roast chicken with golden, crispy skin and succulent meat, a shoulder of lamb gently roasted until meltingly tender, belly of pork with its irresistible crackling, or a rib of deliciously rare beef with gloriously puffed-up and golden Yorkshire Puddings. It's the much-loved, ultimate family meal, so perfectly British.

Cooking a roast dinner may seem like a lot of work and effort but really it's all about the timings. Once you get them right it's as easy as anything. You just need to prepare some vegetables and meat and let the oven do the work, keeping a watchful eye every now and then, and bringing it all together at the end. Slow roasting is as easy as it gets and very forgiving so perfect for the novice wanting to cook Sunday lunch for family and friends.

It doesn't do to skimp on the Sunday joint. Even if it means cutting back a little during the week, the Sunday roast deserves to be a good one, both in terms of quality of meat and size of joint; especially if family and friends are coming round. But even when I'm only cooking for myself and Rob I still buy a cut of meat or a bird large enough to feed at least four, firstly, if I'm being completely honest, because we're both quite greedy when it comes to satisfying our carnivorous cravings, and secondly because I simply love leftover roast meat. It's a close call but in some ways I prefer picking at a plateful of cold roast beef or pork or the carcass of a chicken – especially the chicken – than eating the roast dinner itself. Many a time Rob has caught me at the fridge, door open, light from inside illuminating my guilty deed. As well as giving me an instant and naughty snack, the leftovers provide Rob and I with lunch the next day, stuffed inside sandwiches, rolls or pittas, and often a second dinner: a chicken risotto, a beef salad or a Shepherd's pie. So it's well worth buying that little bit more than you need.

When you're cooking a weekend lunch for the family remember that what they really want is simple, wholesome food that fills them up and tastes great. Now is not the time for artful, perfect plates of food, it's the time for dishes brought to the table full to the brim that everyone can help themselves to, for second helpings and for honest, homely puddings; all made with love.

# Full English Breakfast

The smell of bacon frying is the smell of Sunday morning. Standing by the hob inhaling salty, bacon-infused steam or, if you're lucky enough to have someone cook it for you, waking up the smell wafting under your nose as you lie in bed, is unbeatable.

Everyone does their own version of the Full English breakfast: some like beans where some insist there should be none, some like fried eggs, others prefer scrambled, and then there's the question of black pudding which, traditional as it may be, I'm personally not so keen on. This is how I like it.

**Suggested quantities per person:**

olive oil
2 fat pork sausages
1 large field mushroom
a small vine of cherry tomatoes
2 thick rashers back bacon
1 egg
100g baked beans

Drizzle a small amount of olive oil into a large, non-stick frying pan and add the sausages. Cook them very slowly over a low heat, turning them occasionally. They'll take about 30–40 minutes and by cooking them slowly like this they'll turn sticky and delicious.

About 10 minutes before the end of the cooking time for the sausages, add the mushroom and tomatoes to the pan – or use another frying pan if you haven't got room for everything. After another 5 minutes add the bacon to the pan and the egg, being careful not to break the yolk as you crack the shell.

While everything else is cooking, place the beans in a small pan and heat the beans over a low heat, making sure that they don't come to the boil, as this will spoil them.

When everything is cooked, place the sausages and bacon on kitchen paper and pat off the excess oil off before putting them on the plate along with the remaining ingredients and eat immediately!

**Cook's note**
As always, the best ingredients will give the best dish. If you use poor quality ingredients you'll get a poor quality breakfast. So choose large free-range eggs, preferably organic; fresh, ripe tomatoes; flavoursome mushrooms; thickly cut bacon and good quality pork sausages from your butcher.

Without a doubt roast chicken with all the trimmings is my favourite meal in the entire world, and the meal I would want as my last. No other meal says home to me quite like this one does. It sooths my soul as it feeds my body. The first thing that comes to me when I think of it is the delicious smell as it roasts, which fills the house and teases as it curls under my nose and makes my tummy ache and my mouth water. It creates one of those wonderful cooking aromas that make a house a home.

Next I think of the golden, crispy skin; my favourite part of the bird and one that I'm always impatient for. I eat it while it's too hot to handle, steam escaping from the meat underneath as I pull it away from the breast, ignoring the silent protests from my hot fingers.

Then I think of the succulent breast meat, the more robust and flavoursome leg meat and of the golden, juicy and buttery meat underneath.

But I think what ultimately makes this roasted bird so dear to me is what it symbolises for me; which is a happy, contented home full of good things.

# Heavenly Roast Chicken

**Serves 4**

1 free-range chicken, preferably
  organic and corn-fed,
  approximately 1.8kg
50g salted butter, softened
  (optional, see Cook's notes)
1 lemon, halved
1 garlic bulb, broken into cloves
  and peeled
a small handful of fresh thyme or
  rosemary
olive oil
1 onion, halved
sea salt and freshly ground black
  pepper

Preheat the oven to 220°C/
fan 200°C/gas mark 7.

If you're using butter carefully
separate the skin from the breast of
the chicken by pulling it away at the
fatter end of the chicken (opposite
the neck/cavity end). Once you've
made a gap between the skin and
breast, put your hand in between
and continue separating it all the
way to the top, taking care not to
make a hole in the other end.
Stuff the butter under the skin and
press down on the skin to evenly
distribute the butter over the breast.

Put half of the lemon inside the
cavity of the chicken, followed by
the garlic, thyme or rosemary and
finally the second half of the lemon,
cut end first, to 'seal' the cavity.

Smear olive oil over the breasts
and legs (even if you've used butter
under the skin) as it's going into
a hot oven and you don't want the
skin to dry out and blister. Season
the chicken well with salt and

pepper and put it into a roasting tray
along with the onion, which will
make a great base for a delicious
gravy once it's roasted.

Roast the chicken for 20 minutes.
After this time reduce the temperature
to 190°C/fan 170°C/gas mark 5, take
the chicken out of the oven and baste
it by tilting the tray to allow the fat to
congregate at one end and spooning
it over the breast and legs. Put the
chicken back into the oven and cook
it for a further hour or until it's
completely cooked through and the
juices run clear (see Cook's notes).

Leave the chicken to rest for at least
15 minutes before serving, covered
with foil to keep it warm. If you rest
the chicken breast-side down the
juices will run through the breast
leaving it lovely and moist. If you
like the crispy skin on the chicken,
as I do, remove it from the chicken
before you turn it upside down and
cover it with foil, as the steam from
the chicken will soften up the skin.

While the chicken is resting make
the gravy, using the juices from
the roasting tray and the onion
(see recipe on page 154).

## Cook's notes

The butter under the skin makes the
breast meat deliciously moist as it
melts and seeps into the flesh but
you don't have to use it. If you prefer
a healthier option; the chicken is still
very good without it.

The chicken needs to be at room
temperature when it goes into the
oven and it is cooked when the
juices run completely clear. I find

the best way of checking this is to
take a skewer or knife and split the
skin between the breast and leg and
look down into the gap, as lots of
juices collect there. You can also
skewer the thick part of the thigh
and press down on the meat to allow
the juices to come up through the
hole you've created, or carefully lift
the chicken out of the roasting tray
and hold it vertically over the tray to
allow the juices to come out. If the
juices are not running clear after the
cooking time is up put the chicken
back into the oven for about 15
minutes and then check again.

Carrots are delicious roasted in the
same tray as the chicken as they
soak up the delicious buttery juices.
Simply scrub some carrots, slice
them lengthways then cut the
lengths into halves or quarters,
depending on how long they are
and pop them into the roasting tray
when you turn the temperature
down. Alternatively roast them in
the same tray as the roast potatoes,
if you're making them, or in a tray
all on their own, with a little olive
oil drizzled over them.

If I'm making roast potatoes (see
recipe on page 152) to have with the
chicken I parboil and drain them in
the usual way then put them into the
oven when the temperature is turned
down to 190°C/fan 170°C/gas mark 5,
in a separate roasting tray to the one
the chicken's in. They get an hour at
this temperature while the chicken
is cooking and if they need crisping
up at the end I turn the temperature
up (to about 220°C/fan 200°C/gas
mark 7) to finish them off when the
chicken is removed from the oven.

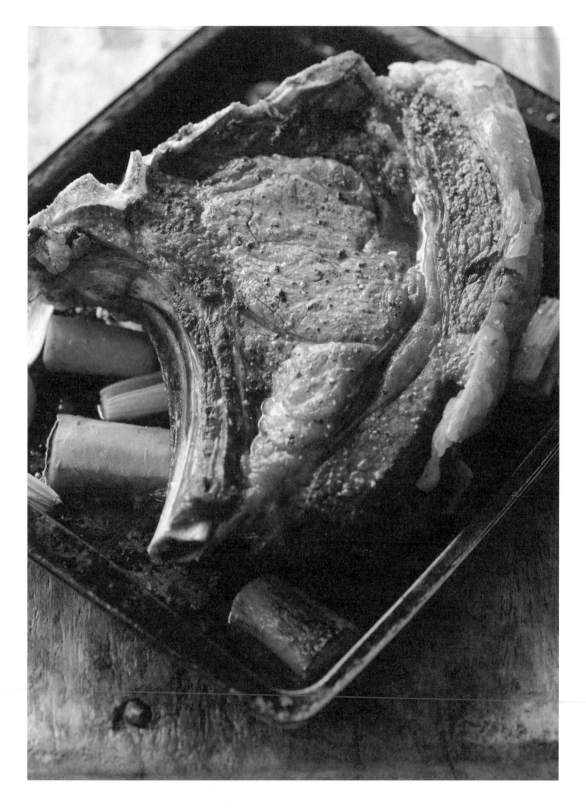

# Roast Rib of Beef

Roast rib of beef is the ultimate British Sunday lunch. It's an expensive cut but it really is worth it, particularly for a special occasion. It's wonderful served with a dark green vegetable such as cabbage or broccoli and of course roast potatoes (see recipe on page 152) and Yorkshire puddings (see recipe on page 153) are a must.

**Serves 4**

rib of beef, approximately 1.5kg
olive oil
1 onion, quartered
2 carrots, roughly chopped
2 celery sticks, roughly chopped
sea salt and freshly ground black
   pepper

Preheat the oven to 240°C/ fan 220°C/gas mark 9.

Rub the beef with the olive oil and season it well with salt and pepper. Put it into a roasting tin along with the onion, carrots and celery – the vegetables will form the base for the gravy.

Cook the beef for 15 minutes then turn the oven down to 190°C/ fan 170°C/gas mark 5 and cook the beef for 15 minutes per 500g, so 45 minutes for a 1.5kg rib. These timings will give you rare beef, which is just how I like it, but cook it for longer if you prefer.

Once the beef has cooked it's important to leave it to rest for at least 15 minutes so that all those lovely juices can seep back into the meat. Covered with foil to keep it warm it will happily sit for half an hour.

Make the gravy with the juices and vegetables left in the roasting tray, following the recipe on page 154.

# Crispy and Fluffy Roast Potatoes

Few people can resist a hot, golden, roast potato that's crispy on the outside and fluffy on the inside. Forget the complex creations of top chefs, if you can master the roast potato you will be considered a culinary expert by your friends and family!

The good news is that making great roast potatoes is easy to do, if you follow a few golden rules, which I describe below.

I have one extra tip for you: make more than you think you'll need; people always want a second helping of good roast potatoes and in my experience the last one in the serving dish will always get eaten – sometimes even fought over!

**Serves 4**

100g fat (see Golden rules for
    perfect roasties) or 100ml olive oil
1kg floury white potatoes, preferably
    King Edwards or Maris Pipers
sea salt

Preheat the oven to 220°C/
fan 200°C/gas mark 7.

Put the fat or oil into a large roasting tray and place it on the highest shelf of the oven to get the fat nice and hot.

While the fat is heating up, peel the potatoes and cut them into halves or quarters, depending on how large they are. I like my roast potatoes fairly large but you can cut them smaller if you prefer – the key thing is to keep them roughly the same size.

Put the potatoes into a pan full of enough cold water to completely cover them. Add a few generous sprinklings of sea salt to the water and bring it to the boil. Cook the potatoes for 8–10 minutes until they're almost, but not completely, cooked through. Drain them immediately in a colander – don't leave them in the water or they'll start to disintegrate – and leave them to dry out for about 5 minutes, which will make them crispier. After this time carefully shake them in the colander, just to rough up their edges. Alternatively use a fork to drag along their edges to rough them up. You just want to take the smoothness off the potatoes to help them crisp up in the oven.

Carefully remove the tray containing the fat out of the oven and lower the potatoes into it (I use a large metal spoon for this to avoid splashes from the hot fat). If the fat is hot enough the potatoes will sizzle when they go into it. Space them out a little in the tray so that they're not touching each other and spoon the fat over the tops so that they're covered in it.

Return the tray to the oven and roast the potatoes for 50–60 minutes, until they're crispy and golden all over. Turn them once or twice during cooking to get them evenly golden. Don't turn them until they've crisped up underneath, or they'll stick to the bottom of the tray. If they don't come away from the tray easily when you try to turn them, they're not ready to be turned.

Lay the potatoes onto kitchen paper and dab off any excess fat before serving them straight away.

**Golden rules for perfect roasties**

*1.* Use floury potatoes. Choosing the right potato is the important starting point. You want a good floury one such as King Edward or Maris Piper.

*2.* Parboil the potatoes. Parboiling the potatoes before you roast them is what gives them that fluffy inside, as they've already started to cook in the middle before they go into the oven. You don't need to parboil them for long – you're not cooking them through – just partly cooking them so that a knife will easily pierce them but not go right through.

*3.* Choose a good fat and make sure it's sizzling hot when the potatoes go in. The optimum fat to use is goose fat, which will make your potatoes taste amazing. I tend to save this for special occasions though, such as Christmas, to save the arteries. You can also use duck fat or beef dripping, both of which will also make your potatoes taste incredibly good. For a healthier option you can use olive oil and still get good results. Whichever fat you use, put it into the roasting tin and into a hot oven to heat up before you add your potatoes. Make sure it's really hot; you want a nice sizzle when you add the potatoes.

*4.* Roast the potatoes in a hot oven. Roast potatoes need a good blast of heat to crisp them up, so make sure your oven is nice and hot before they go in.

# Yorkshire Puddings

I've discovered over the years that the secret to good Yorkshire Puddings is a hat trick: three things which, combined, will give you beautifully risen Yorkshire puddings.

First things first, leave the batter to rest once you've mixed it up, for at least half an hour. Second – and this is very important – you need to get the fat in the tray hot, and I mean really hot. It should sizzle when you pour the batter in and you should see the batter instantly start to react and cook before it's even in the oven. The final thing is this: whatever you do, do not open the oven door until the puddings are ready, not even a fraction for a peek. The rush of cold air may prevent the Yorkshire puddings from rising, or collapse if they already have. You have been warned!

**Makes 4 puddings**

110g plain flour
2 eggs
150ml semi-skimmed milk
2 tablespoons fat such as beef
    dripping or olive oil
salt

Put the flour into a bowl with a pinch of salt, then make a dip in the middle. Beat the eggs and milk together in a jug then slowly pour it into the dip you made in the flour, gradually incorporating it into the flour with a whisk as you pour. Continue to whisk it until you have a smooth batter then leave it to rest for 30 minutes.

Preheat the oven to 220°C/ fan 200°C/gas mark 7.

Put half a tablespoon of fat or oil into each of the four cases in a Yorkshire pudding tray and then put the tray into the oven for 15 minutes.

Once the fat or oil is sizzling hot pour the batter evenly into each of the cases. Put the tray back into the oven and leave the puddings to cook for 20–25 minutes, until they are risen, puffy and golden.

**Cook's note**
This recipe makes 4 puddings but it can easily be doubled if there are more of you for dinner.

# Gravy

Home-made gravy is so simple and yet so very special. It's the make or break of a good roast dinner and once you've mastered it you'll never want to use gravy granules again.

Here are the elements and steps for making gravy for roasted meat:

*The roasting tray*
The tray you roast the meat in will go on the hob when you start making the gravy so a metal tray is best. If you're using gas make sure the tray is flameproof and avoid Pyrex and earthenware. In my early cooking years I broke a couple of dishes this way with a big bang as they cracked so beware!

*Vegetables*
I often throw in a quartered onion with the meat as it roasts to give the gravy a good onion base. You can also add use other vegetables to the onion such as carrots and celery; this all adds to the all-important flavour so the more the merrier. Garlic can be good too but remember this is a strong flavour so will be quite dominant in the gravy.

Once the meat is cooked remove it from the roasting tray and place the tray on the hob. Leave the vegetables you've used for your gravy in the tray at this point.

*Remove excess fat*
Spoon off most of the fat until you're left with about a tablespoon, making sure you don't remove the precious juices from the meat. The best way to do this is to tilt the tray so that all the juices and fat are in one corner. The fat is lighter and sits on top of the darker juices so you should be able to easily see it to remove it.

*Thickening*
I don't always add flour, sometimes just adding the thin meat juices to the roast, but if I want a fairly thick gravy I will add a tablespoon or two of plain flour to the tray now. Stir it well over a low to medium heat, whilst dislodging all the crusty bits from the tray with your spoon – they contain lots of delicious flavour. It will look sludgy and horrible but that's exactly how it should look.

*Liquid*
When the flour is well mixed in and you can't see it any more, and you've dislodged all the crusty bits from the tray, it's time to add your liquid. Depending on the meat you are serving, what you have in your storecupboard, and your personal taste, you could add a glass of wine, port, Madeira or Marsala. You don't have to add alcohol but it does give a good flavour to the gravy. I rarely add alcohol to chicken gravy as I find it doesn't need it – the chicken juices usually give enough flavour if I'm using a good organic chicken – but occasionally I might add a glass of white wine. Worcestershire Sauce is also good to add flavour if the gravy needs something extra.

You also add stock or vegetable cooking water at this stage or even just water if the gravy has enough flavour. Again I find chicken gravy usually has enough flavour so I just use water but other meats sometimes need a helping hand. You can add as much or as little stock or water as you like depending on how much gravy you want.

Once you've added your liquid bring it to a simmer and keep stirring everything around until it's well combined. Press on the vegetables with your spoon so that they release their juices.

*Reduce*
Now keep simmering and tasting until you're happy with the consistency and flavour.

*Strain and serve*
Strain the gravy through a sieve into a jug and serve.

It's that simple and takes very little time. When you've made it once or twice you'll be able to do it without even thinking!

# Carrot and Swede Mash

I love this sweet vegetable mash and it tends to be a hit with children too. It's particularly good with roast chicken.

**Serves 4**

½ swede, approximately 500g
500g carrots
a knob of butter
sea salt and freshly ground black
    pepper

Cut the vegetables into large dice, roughly the same size. Add them to a large pan of water then bring it to the boil and cook the vegetables, for approximately 15–20 minutes or until tender.

Once cooked, drain the vegetables and then mash them with the butter and some salt and black pepper. You can either mash them until fairly smooth or keep them a little chunky for more texture. Check the seasoning before serving as a side dish.

**Cook's notes**
The amount of swede and carrots are listed as a suggestion; you could use any amount as long as you have roughly the same amount of each.

Other combinations of root vegetables work just as well – I particularly like parsnips with the carrots and swede.

# Pot Roast Beef Brisket

This is a great winter dish with meltingly tender vegetables, flavoursome beef and a strong, rich gravy. Brisket requires long, slow cooking, but it's full of flavour and well worth waiting for. You can vary the root vegetables as you like.

**Serves 4–6**

olive oil
a joint of beef brisket, rolled and
    tied with string, approximately
    1.5 kg
6 small shallots, peeled and left
    whole
2 garlic cloves, finely sliced
400ml beef stock or 200ml beef
    stock and 200ml red wine
4–6 carrots, roughly chopped
1 small swede, cut into chunks
a few sprigs of fresh thyme

sea salt and freshly ground black
    pepper
boiled or mashed potatoes, to serve

Preheat the oven to 150°C/
fan 130°C/gas mark 2.

Drizzle a little olive oil into a flameproof casserole dish and heat it over a high heat. Season the beef well then add it to the dish and brown it on all sides. Add the shallots and garlic and sauté them for a couple of minutes then add the remaining ingredients and bring to the boil. Cover the dish with a lid and put it in the oven to cook for around 3–4 hours until the beef is tender, turning it a few times during the cooking time.

If the gravy needs thickening up at the end of the cooking time remove the beef and vegetables from the dish then put it onto the hob and simmer it until it reduces and thickens. Check the seasoning before serving slices of the beef with some of the vegetables and gravy. Boiled or mashed potatoes are good to serve with it too.

# Alchemy in the Kitchen: Chicken Stock or Broth

I adore home-made chicken stock and love making it. As it simmers slowly the house is filled with its wonderful smell, making it feel happy and homely. Something wonderful begins to happen as the goodness and the flavour from the chicken bones and vegetables seep into the water.

You simply can't beat using your own home-made stock in risottos and soups where the base stock is particularly important for the flavour of the finished dish.

More often than not though, it doesn't actually make it as stock in my house as I can't resist having a bowlful just as it is. Lightly seasoned with sea salt and sometimes served with slices of chicken, the soothing broth is heavenly and healing. I believe in its magic.

1 chicken carcass
2 celery sticks, roughly chopped
1 carrot, roughly chopped,
1 large onion, halved
1 leek, roughly chopped
1 bay leaf
a few sprigs of fresh parsley and
    thyme
6 peppercorns
sea salt

Remove any garlic, lemon or herbs from the cavity of the chicken carcass. Put the carcass into a large pan, along with the vegetables, herbs and peppercorns, and just cover it with water.

Bring the water to the boil then very gently simmer it on the lowest heat for about 2 hours. Remove any scum that comes to the surface during this time.

After 2 hours sieve the stock into a clean pan. Increase the heat and allow the stock to reduce until you're happy with the flavour.

If serving as broth season with salt before serving.

**Cook's note**
Stock freezes well and it's very handy to keep in your freezer. I usually freeze it in volumes of 500ml or 1 litre so I can take out just the amount I need. Defrost the stock thoroughly before using and don't re-freeze it.

## Slow roasting

There's something very primitive about putting a slab of meat into the oven and cooking it very gently and slowly all day long. I derive great pleasure and comfort out of knowing it's there and being enticed by its incredible smell as it cooks.

What's great about this style of cooking is that it's so easy and you don't need to watch the clock; you can just put whatever spices, herbs and vegetables you like into a roasting tin with the meat, add some liquid, put it in the oven and leave it. It will stay there until you're ready for it; just top it up with liquid as needed and turn the temperature down a little if you want to leave it in the oven for longer.

The kind of cuts most suited to slow cooking – the cheaper, fattier cuts – are often the most flavoursome and so not only is it the easiest kind of roasting but it's also the most rewarding in terms of taste; what could be better?

Slow roasting has come back into favour in recent years and perhaps one downside of this popularity is that the cheaper cuts of meat are not quite as cheap as they once were. But none the less this is still a thrifty way of cooking, particularly as you can use up whatever vegetables are sitting in your fridge, and you can certainly feed a crowd easily and without breaking the bank.

# Slow Roasted Belly of Pork

Belly of pork has become quite fashionable in recent years, finding itself on the menus of London's top restaurants, and yet it's a homely dish through and through; there's nothing fancy about it, nothing artful to be done with it, it's just simple, wholesome food. Like most of the cheaper, fattier cuts of meat, pork belly is an incredibly flavoursome cut of meat and when cooked slowly it's meltingly tender. Don't worry too much about the fat; most of it cooks away and what's left just adds to the flavour.

There are two elements to the way I cook this dish: first the dry skin and high heat for crispy crackling and secondly stock to create tender meat. Although the stock creates some steam, as the heat is fairly low and the skin has already had a chance to crisp up in the hot oven the crackling isn't too affected. But if you find it isn't as crisp as you'd like it at the end of the cooking time simply cut it away from the pork and put it back in the oven at full whack to really crisp it up.

**Serves 4–6**

1 piece of belly pork,
    approximately 1.5kg
800ml chicken stock
1 large onion, quartered
2 garlic cloves, sliced
2 celery sticks, roughly chopped
2 carrots, roughly chopped
1 bay leaf
3 or 4 sprigs of fresh thyme
sea salt
steamed cabbage and mashed
    potato, to serve

Preheat the oven to 230°C/ fan 210°C/gas mark 8.

Score the skin of the pork with a sharp knife or, preferably, get your butcher to do it for you. Pat the skin dry with kitchen paper then rub it with sea salt. Put the pork into a roasting tin and into the oven.

After 30 minutes remove any fat from the roasting tin and pour the chicken stock around the pork, making sure it doesn't touch the skin as that needs to stay dry. Add the onion, garlic cloves, celery and carrots to the tin along with the herbs. Make sure the herbs are fully immersed in the stock otherwise they'll just dry out in the oven.

Reduce the oven temperature to 150°C/fan 130°C/gas mark 2 and cook the pork for a further 2½ hours by which time it should be very tender. You shouldn't need to top up the stock during the cooking time but check it once or twice and if it does run low top it up with a little more stock or water.

If the cracking isn't as crispy as you would like at the end of the cooking time carefully cut it away from the pork, turn the heat back up to 230°C/fan 210°C/gas mark 8 and put the crackling back into the oven to crisp it up.

Skim any excess fat off the juices and serve them with the pork. If they're too thin for your liking put the roasting tin on the hob,

bring them up to the boil and simmer them to reduce them down a little.

The pork is great served with simply steamed cabbage and mashed potato to soak up all the juices.

**Cook's note**
Belly of pork is, as you would expect, cut from the underside of the pig and it's the cut used to make streaky bacon and Italian pancetta. It's also the cut that spare ribs comes from. It is a fatty cut but when you roast it slowly over a few hours most of the fat renders away leaving you with wonderfully succulent and flavoursome meat.

# Slow Lamb

We generally associate lamb with the springtime but it's even nicer and more flavoursome in the autumn, when it's a little older and had longer to graze and develop. And at this time of year, when it starts turning cooler, it's absolutely fantastic to slowly roast a shoulder of lamb with red wine, stock and vegetables.

If you have any of this lamb left over it's great served in warmed pitta bread and quite spectacular in a Shepherd's Pie (see recipe on page 163); in fact it's worth cooking more than you need just for this purpose.

**Serves 4–6**

olive oil
1 bone-in shoulder of lamb,
    weighing approximately 1.5kg
400ml red wine
200ml lamb or chicken stock
a few sprigs of fresh rosemary
2 onions, halved
2 garlic cloves, crushed
sea salt and freshly ground black
    pepper
steamed or sautéed cabbage and
    mashed potato, to serve

Preheat the oven to 220°C/ fan 200°C/gas mark 7.

Rub a little olive oil over the lamb and season it well, then put it into a roasting tin and into the oven for about 20 minutes until browned, turning once.

Reduce the oven temperature to 150°C/fan 130°C/gas mark 2 and add the wine, stock, rosemary, onions and garlic to the tin. Return the lamb to the oven for a further 4 hours, after which time it will have soaked up all the wine and stock and should be meltingly tender.

Serve the lamb with cabbage and mashed potatoes.

# Spaghetti Bolognese

As in many British households, this dish, the British take on the Italian ragù sauce, was a regular and firm favourite with my family when I was growing up and I still enjoy it today. I've developed this recipe over the years through adjusting and tweaking it each time I made it and now I have a trusty recipe that gives a thick, rich, flavoursome sauce just how I like it. It's cooked very slowly for a few hours which allows the flavours to really develop and the mince to become very tender.

The key to this particular recipe is my secret ingredient, port, which came to be in it because one day I had no red wine so I used the closest thing I had. This of course just demonstrates that often the best recipes come about through chance and accident. The port gives the sauce a deep richness quite different to what you get with wine. I liked the result so much I permanently replaced the wine with port in my recipe. However, if you prefer the more traditional taste by all means use a good red wine instead.

**Serves 4**

**For the sauce**
500g lean beef mince
60g pancetta, finely diced
1 onion, finely diced
1 celery stick, finely diced
1 carrot, finely diced
1 garlic clove, crushed
250ml port
400g can chopped tomatoes
250ml beef stock
a couple of dashes of Worcestershire sauce

a sprig of fresh thyme
1 bay leaf
1–2 teaspoon dried oregano
1–2 tablespoons tomato purée

400g spaghetti
sea salt and freshly ground black pepper
Parmesan cheese, to serve

Brown the mince in a large non-stick pan over a high heat until it forms a dark brown crust; this is really important as it adds so much to the flavour. Drain any liquid that is released from the mince, as this will stop it browning well. Once browned, remove the mince from the pan and set aside.

In the same pan sauté the pancetta until it releases its fat and starts to colour, then add the onion, celery, carrot and garlic. Once the vegetables have softened and taken on a light colour return the mince to the pan.

Add the port, the chopped tomatoes, beef stock, Worcestershire sauce, whole thyme sprig, bay leaf, dried oregano and tomato purée.

Bring the sauce to the boil then turn the heat right down and let it very gently simmer for a couple of hours, adding a little water if it starts to go dry. It should be only barely simmering with just the occasional bubble rising to the surface every now and then. This way it will cook nice and slowly which will develop the flavours and tenderise the meat.

Once the sauce is thick and the mince tender, cook the spaghetti. Bring a large pan of salted water to the boil then add the spaghetti. Bring the water back up to the boil and cook the spaghetti according to the pack instructions, until *al dente* – soft on the outside but still a little firm in the middle.

Once the spaghetti is cooked drain it and divide it among 4 plates. Season the sauce to taste then remove the sprig of thyme and the bay leaf. Top the spaghetti with the sauce and serve it with Parmesan cheese to be generously grated over.

**Cook's notes**
Chop the vegetables very finely as there's nothing worse than big pieces of carrot or celery in the sauce.

For a change try using half beef and half pork mince, which is often used in the traditional Italian ragù sauce.

To brown the mince, I find it's easier to keep it in one block when it's all still compacted together, and brown it over a very high heat, then turn it over, brown it on that side, and then break it up and brown it some more. The trick for getting a brown crust is not to move the mince around the pan as it browns but leave it alone to form the crust, and also to drain out any liquid that's released from the mince as it cooks.

In Italy it's common to mix the sauce through the pasta but when I was growing up the sauce was always dolloped on top and so it's through fond nostalgia that I do the same.

# Toad in the Hole

When I'm in the mood for Toad in the hole I don't want something light, I want a proper, hearty dish, with thick, puffy and crispy batter, which is what this version gives me. However, if you do prefer a lighter batter you can halve the quantity of milk in this recipe and make up the other half with water. I like to serve this with onion gravy – see Cook's note for the recipe.

**Serves 4**

225g plain flour
4 eggs
300ml semi-skimmed milk
8 pork sausages
olive oil
2 tablespoons fat such as beef
   dripping, or olive oil
salt

Preheat the oven to 220°C/ fan 200°C/gas mark 7.

Put the flour into a large mixing bowl, stir in a pinch of salt and then make a dip in the middle. Beat the eggs and milk together in a jug then slowly pour it into the dip you made in the flour, gradually incorporating it into the flour with a whisk as you pour. Continue to whisk it until you have a smooth batter then leave it to rest for 30 minutes.

While the batter is resting, heat a little olive oil in a frying pan and brown the sausages, then set them aside.

When the batter has been resting for 15 minutes put the fat or oil into a non-stick roasting tin approximately 30 x 24cm and then put it into the oven to heat it up for 15 minutes while the batter continues to rest. After 15 minutes pour the batter into the tin and then add the sausages, allowing a gap between them to allow the batter to rise up around them.

Put the tin back into the oven and leave it to cook for 30–35 minutes, until the batter is risen, puffy and golden. It's important that you don't open the oven door until the end of the cooking time or the batter may not rise, or collapse if it already has.

**Cook's note**
This is nice served with onion gravy: Put a knob of butter into a medium pan or small non-stick frying pan along with a little olive oil and melt it over a low heat. Add 3–4 halved and sliced onions and cook them gently, stirring occasionally, for about 40 minutes so that they slowly turn soft and golden. Then sprinkle in a tablespoon of plain flour and stir well with a wooden spoon. Gradually add enough beef stock to reach the required amount of gravy, stirring continuously. Once you've added the stock bring it to the boil and simmer it, stirring occasionally, until it thickens. Season to taste and serve with the Toad in the hole.

# Shepherd's Pie

There's often confusion between Shepherd's pie and Cottage pie but the difference is quite simple: they are more or less the same dish except that Shepherd's pie is made with lamb and Cottage pie is made with beef. Therefore, although this recipe is specifically shepherd's pie, you could easily substitute the lamb for beef and make cottage pie.

**Serves 4**

**For the filling**
500g raw lamb mince or 500g
   cooked lamb, cut into bite-sized
   pieces
1 onion, finely diced
1 celery stick, finely diced
1 carrot, finely diced
1 garlic clove, crushed
olive oil
1 tablespoon plain flour
400ml lamb or chicken stock
1 tablespoon tomato purée
a couple of dashes of Worcestershire sauce
2 sprigs of fresh thyme
sea salt and freshly ground black
   pepper

**For the topping**
1kg floury potatoes such as Maris
   Piper or King Edwards, cut into
   even-sized chunks
50g butter

Preheat the oven to 200°C/ fan 180°C/gas mark 6.

If using raw lamb mince, brown it in a large non-stick pan over a high heat so that it forms a dark crust. Pour any liquid and excess fat out of the pan as it renders out of the mince, otherwise it won't brown as well. Remove the lamb from the pan once it's browned and set aside.

Remove any excess fat from the pan, leaving about a tablespoon, then fry the onion, celery, carrot and garlic until softened, but not coloured, adding a little olive oil if necessary. Sprinkle over the flour and mix it well then add the lamb, stock, tomato purée and Worces-tershire sauce. Add the leaves from the sprigs of thyme and stir everything well. Bring it up to a gentle simmer and cook for about 20–30 minutes, until it thickens up nicely.

While the filling is simmering, cook the potatoes. Place the chunks into a large pan of salted water. Bring the water to the boil and cook the potatoes until tender. Drain them and mash them with the butter.

Once the lamb filling has thickened up, season it to taste then put it into a 22cm round, 8 cm deep ovenproof dish. Top with the potato then drag a fork along the top horizontally and vertically. This will make it crisp up nicely in the oven. Bake the pie for about 35–40 minutes until bubbling and golden.

**Cook's note**
I prefer to make this with leftover roast lamb, it's so much more flavoursome, especially slow roasted lamb such as the recipe on page 160. If you don't have enough leftover lamb bump it up with a leg of lamb steak, diced and fried until cooked through.

# Plum Crumble

You can't beat a good crumble and this one is my absolute favourite. Hot, jammy plums are absolutely delicious under the biscuity topping, making this a real rib-sticking, soul-soothing pudding. Sometimes I like to throw in a couple of handfuls of blackberries with the plums to ring the changes.

**Serves 4**

**For the filling**
800g ripe plums, stoned and
    quartered
40–60g caster sugar, depending on
    how sweet the plums are

**For the topping**
240g plain flour
140g butter
80g caster sugar
double cream, Home-made Custard
    (see page 166) or vanilla ice
    cream, to serve

Preheat the oven to 200°C/fan 180°C/Gas Mark 6.

Put the plum quarters into a 22cm round or square, 8 cm deep ovenproof dish and sprinkle them with caster sugar, then toss the plums in it so that they get nicely coated.

Put the flour, butter and sugar into a medium mixing bowl and rub together between your fingers until the mixture takes on the texture of biscuit or cake crumbs.

Sprinkle the crumbly topping over the fruit, covering it entirely. Don't press down on the topping; keep it loose.

Bake for 30–40 minutes or until the fruit is bubbling and the top is lightly golden. Serve with double cream, Home-made Custard or ice cream.

# Home-made Custard

For years I never made my own custard as I thought it was too time consuming, too difficult and too much hassle. So when I did finally make it I was surprised by how quick and easy it actually is. It's simply a case of beating some egg yolks, cornflour and sugar together, heating some milk and cream with a vanilla pod, combining them and then thickening up the mixture on the hob. The resulting thick, creamy vanilla custard is delicious, and when your family pours it over their puddings and exclaims at how good it is you'll be as pleased as punch that you went to the effort of making it yourself.

**Makes approximately 700ml**

4 egg yolks
40g caster sugar
1 teaspoon cornflour
300ml full fat milk
300ml double cream
1 vanilla pod

Place the egg yolks, sugar and cornflour in a medium mixing bowl and beat them together until they are a pale yellow. Set it aside.

Pour the milk and cream into a small non-stick pan. Split the vanilla pod lengthways with a knife then run the back of the knife along the middle of the pod – down both sides – to take out all the gorgeous seeds and add them to the pan along with the pod. Heat the milk and cream to just below boiling point and then take it off the heat.

Add the heated milk and cream to the egg, sugar and cornflour mixture in the bowl and stir it together then pour it into a clean small non-stick pan. You could use the same pan if you wanted to save on the washing up but it's nicer to use a fresh one so that it doesn't have all the milk and cream residue in it. Add the vanilla pod to the pan then heat the mixture, stirring all the time, until it thickens up. Remove the vanilla pod before serving.

# Baked Apples

Baked apples are a very English, very homely pudding; the kind that mums make. When someone gives you one you feel truly loved.

I find it best to use eating, rather than cooking apples, as they can quickly turn to mush in the oven. I like whisky-drenched sultanas mixed with the fudgy light muscovado sugar but you could use brandy instead or alternatively skip the alcohol altogether.

**Serves 4**

30g sultanas
2 tablespoons whisky
30g light muscovado or other
    brown sugar
30g butter
4 eating apples
Home-made Custard (see page 166),
    cream or vanilla ice cream, to
    serve

Pour the whisky over the sultanas and leave them to soak in it for at least an hour, but the longer the better.

When you're ready to bake the apples mix the soaked sultanas, along with any whisky they haven't soaked up, with the sugar and butter.

Preheat the oven to 180°C/ fan 160°C/gas mark 4. Line a baking tray with baking parchment.

Core the apples and fill the centres with the raisins and butter mixture, piling any excess mixture on top of each apple.

Put the apples onto the lined baking tray. Bake them until they're soft but not collapsed, which should take about 30 minutes but check them after 20 minutes as small apples won't take so long. Baste them with the buttery juices half way through the cooking time.

Serve the apples with custard, cream or ice cream

# Honey and Banana Pancakes

Pancakes are great fun to make, and they're not just for Pancake day. The filling possibilities are endless but I like this simple warm banana and honey filling, which is wholesome and delicious.

**Makes 4 pancakes**

**For the pancakes**
60g plain flour
1 large egg
150ml milk
vegetable oil, for cooking

**For the filling**
2 bananas
1–2 tablespoons clear honey

To make the batter, sift the flour into a medium mixing bowl and make a well in the centre, then crack the egg into it. Whisk the egg, gradually incorporating the flour until it starts to form a paste and then slowly whisk in the milk so that you get a smooth mixture the consistency of single cream. Leave the batter to stand for 30 minutes.

When you're ready to make the pancakes slice the bananas and put them into a small non-stick pan with the honey and heat gently. As the honey starts to loosen spoon it over the bananas to coat them in it and then take the pan off the heat. Keep the mixture warm by covering it with a lid or foil while you make the pancakes.

To make the pancakes brush a little oil onto the base of an 18–20cm frying pan using a pastry brush. Heat the pan over a high heat so that it's nice and hot and then turn the heat down to medium. Add a ladleful of batter to the pan and swirl it around so that it covers the bottom of the pan. Cook for a minute or two until the bottom of the pancake starts to turn golden. You can check this by loosening the edges with a palette knife and checking underneath. When the bottom of the pancake is cooked flip it over with the palette knife or by tossing it in the air. The other side won't take as long to cook, only about 30–60 seconds.

When the pancake is cooked transfer it to a warmed plate. Spoon some of the banana mixture into the middle of the pancake and fold it over. Cover the pancake with foil to keep hot while you cook the remaining pancakes.

Repeat to make the remaining pancakes, brushing a little more oil onto the bottom of the frying pan each time to prevent the pancakes from sticking.

Oh the weather outside is frightful,
But the fire is so delightful,
And since we've no place to go,
Let it snow! Let it snow! Let it snow!

Sammy Cahn

# snow flurries

Toward the end of October the clocks go back, signalling the transition into winter, and as the weeks move on the nights get colder and darker. For me, the descent of winter always seems to happen quite suddenly; there I am one minute fully immersed in the spirit of autumn, enjoying the festivities of Halloween and Bonfire night and marvelling at the colour of the leaves, the next hunting for my gloves and scarf as the bare trees bend in the wind outside. The first cold snap is always a shock to my system; I don't like the cold and no matter how I wrap up it always manages to penetrate, making my fingers numb and my ears ache. I think perhaps I was meant to be a hibernating creature, snugly sleeping through the winter months until the spring sunshine gently coaxes me out of my warm burrow and into the world again.

Of course I love the romantic notion of winter: battening down the hatches when it's dark and cold outside on a crisp winter night; sipping hot chocolate under a blanket in front of a crackling log fire and flickering candles; serenely walking through thick, powder-soft snow as it gently flutters down.

Sadly those kinds of winters tend only to happen in my head, but still, I dream, and I hold on to that fantasy as winter descends. On cold, cold nights I take long, hot baths scented with my favourite rose oil before wrapping myself in a large, fluffy towel, climbing into soft, warm pyjamas and sinking into a freshly laundered bed. I pull on thick bed socks to keep my toes toasty warm and I hug a hot water bottle. Then I pick up a book from my bedside table and lose myself in it, letting it transport me to a faraway place and introduce me to captivating characters. It's a child-like ritual, one that's immensely comforting and one that helps me through the winter journey.

At this time of year not only do I want to be wrapped up warm and snug inside, but I want to stock up on good things to eat; that hibernating instinct again. I like knowing that if ever I were to find myself in the highly unlikely situation of being snowed in here in the south east of London, I would be perfectly comfortable for days on end with my packed fridge and good things stashed away in my cupboards. I do actually recall being literally snowed in once

during my childhood in the Medway Towns. We could hardly see out of the kitchen window for snow and our neighbour had to use a shovel to clear a path to our front door; all terribly exciting for a child. Particularly exciting was listening intently to the local radio in the morning with my mum and my sister to see if our school would be included in the long list of those that were closed due to the snow. Certainly this nostalgia is in part an explanation of my desire to stock up and bolt up, but then I think all lovers of good food and all homemakers have that same nesting instinct to some extent.

When the skies are heavy with snow or slate-grey with a swirling wind, it's the food cupboards that I turn to and the treasures within: the slabs of the finest quality chocolate – dark, white, spiced – neatly lined up in their foil and paper wrappers; the glass jar containing white caster sugar and vanilla pods that engulfs me with its dreamy sweet smell each time I pop open the lid; the cotton bag of Arborio rice that feels like little pearls running through my fingers. The wintry weather can stay as long as it likes...

# Chorizo and Savoy Cabbage Risotto

I love this colourful and mildly spicy risotto in the winter when I want some warmth and cheer; it brings summer back for a fleeting moment. The crunch and deep flavour of the Savoy cabbage is robust enough to stand up to the chorizo and the rice marries them together in perfect harmony.

**Serves 4**

1.5 litre chicken stock
250g fresh uncooked chorizo
    sausage, skinned and diced
1 onion, finely diced
300g risotto rice, such as Arborio
100ml dry vermouth
6 Savoy cabbage leaves, shredded
    into bite-sized pieces
sea salt and freshly ground black
    pepper
grated Parmesan cheese, to serve
    (optional)

Heat the stock in a medium pan until it is hot but not simmering, ready to ladle into the risotto.

Sauté the diced chorizo in a large, non-stick, dry frying pan over a medium heat until it's cooked through. Remove it with a slotted spoon, leaving the oil that comes out of the chorizo in the pan.

Next, add the onion to the pan and sauté it for a couple of minutes, coating it in the oil that has been released from the chorizo. Add the rice and stir well, coating it in the oil, until it starts to turn translucent then pour in the vermouth and stir the rice for about 30 seconds while the alcohol sizzles and burns off.

Start adding the hot stock, one ladleful at time, stirring continuously. Allow the rice to absorb each ladleful before adding the next. About halfway through add the cabbage to the risotto, stirring it in.

Keep adding stock until the rice is *al dente*, not totally soft all the way through but still with a bite in the middle, and the risotto has a sauce-like consistency. Different varieties of rice absorb differing quantities of liquid so you may not need all of the stock, or you may need a little more liquid (topping it up with water is fine).

Add the chorizo towards the end and ensure it's heated through before serving. Season to taste and serve with grated Parmesan cheese if liked.

**Cook's note**
Chorizo is a spicy Spanish sausage made with pork and paprika, which gives it its characteristic smoky, spicy flavour and beautiful red colour. You can get lots of different types, varying in spiciness and flavour. Whichever you choose, make sure it's fresh, uncooked chorizo so that the oil and juices can be released and absorbed by the rice, giving it that all-important flavour.

# Warm Duck and Red Cabbage Salad

I tend to make this salad for a midweek dinner when I've been out at work all day as it's quick and easy and, because the duck is warm and meaty, I still feel like I've had a good, wholesome meal.

I like the crunch of the raw cabbage but it needs to be finely shredded or grated to avoid it being too overbearing in the salad. It works well, both in terms of texture and taste, with the warm duck, succulent with its juices, and the tangy dressing, which pulls everything together and gives the dish a lift.

**Serves 2**

3 handfuls of salad leaves
1 handful of red cabbage, grated or
    very finely shredded
2 duck breasts, skin on
sea salt and freshly ground black
    pepper

**For the dressing**
3 tablespoons extra virgin olive oil
1 tablespoon red wine vinegar

Toss the salad leaves with the red cabbage and divide them between two plates. For the dressing, whisk together the extra virgin olive oil and red wine vinegar and set it aside.

Season the duck breasts then heat a medium, non-stick, dry frying pan over a medium heat and put them into it, skin side down. As they cook they will release their fat into the pan, which you should drain out of the pan and, if you like, save it for roast potatoes another time. Cook the duck breasts for 10 minutes on each side for medium rare, a few minutes less for rare or a few minutes longer for well done. Remove them from the pan and leave them to rest for 5 minutes.

Thickly slice the duck breasts on the diagonal. Drizzle a little dressing over the salads and arrange the duck slices over the salad leaves on the plates.

# Sausage and Lentil Casserole

There's something very reassuring about a bowl of sausages and lentils. It's simple, familiar food that welcomes you home.

**Serves 4**

olive oil
8 sausages
1 onion, finely diced
1 carrot, finely diced
1 celery stick, finely diced
1 garlic clove, crushed
150g dried brown or green lentils
400g can chopped tomatoes
800ml beef stock
1 tablespoon tomato purée
$\frac{1}{2}$ teaspoon dried oregano
sea salt and freshly ground black
    pepper
thick crusty bread, to serve

Preheat the oven to 200°C/
fan 180°C/gas mark 6.

Drizzle a little olive oil into a large flameproof casserole dish and heat it over a medium high heat. Add the sausages and brown them in the oil then remove them and cut them into bite-sized pieces.

Add the onion, carrot, celery and garlic to the pan and sauté them for about 5 minutes over a medium heat, until softened and starting to take on a little colour.

Return the sausages to the dish along with the lentils, tomatoes, stock, tomato purée and oregano then season well. Bring the liquid to the boil then cover and cook in the oven for about 40 minutes, until the lentils are tender and the sausages are cooked through.

The casserole is quite substantial as it is but if you want to serve something with it thick crusty bread would be great.

**Cook's note**
The garlic, dried oregano and black pepper in this recipe combine to give this casserole a warmth that makes it perfect to eat when the icy wind is blowing up a gale outside. Many cooks will tell you that dried herbs are of little value and, whilst I would agree that fresh is usually best, I find that dried oregano adds a deep, pungent and warming back-note to winter stews and casseroles which, in my opinion, makes it well worth keeping in the storecupboard.

# Leek Omelette

Leeks are one of my favourite vegetables; I love their sweet, mild onion flavour; and this omelette, which is finished off under the grill, really shows them off.

**Serves 1**

3 eggs
a knob of butter
1 leek, white and light green parts, finely sliced
a handful of grated Parmesan cheese
sea salt and freshly ground black pepper
green salad, to serve

Preheat the grill to high.

Lightly beat the eggs together with some seasoning and set them aside.

Melt the butter in a non-stick, ovenproof frying pan approximately 20–24cm in diameter then add the leek and sauté it for about 5 minutes until softened.

Arrange the leek in an even layer in the pan then add the beaten eggs to the pan, tilting it and swirling the eggs around so that they coat the bottom of the pan, leaving no gaps. Cook until the bottom has firmed up and the omelette is almost set.

Sprinkle over the grated Parmesan cheese then put the pan under the grill for 2–3 minutes to cook the top of the omelette until it is lightly golden and bubbling. I sometimes like my omelettes with a little green salad on the side but otherwise just eat them as they are.

# Bean and Bacon Soup

This soup is based on my mum's bean and bacon stew, which she used to make for us when we were children and she was cooking on a budget. She used to make a big batch with cans of baked beans and rashers of bacon. We would eat it with bread to dip in and have it again the next day, which was no hardship as we loved it and, as with most stews, casseroles and soups, it was even better reheated the next day.

**Serves 4**

200g smoked back bacon, rind
    removed, chopped into bite-sized
    pieces
olive oil
1 onion, finely diced
2 x 400g cans cannellini beans,
    drained
400g can chopped tomatoes
800ml vegetable stock
sea salt and freshly ground black
    pepper

Sauté the bacon in a large pan over a medium heat until it is well coloured, but don't allow it to turn crispy. You shouldn't need to add any fat as the bacon will release its own fat into the pan, but if there isn't enough add a little olive oil.

Once the bacon is well coloured add the onion and sauté it until it softens. Next, add the cannellini beans, tomatoes and vegetable stock and stir everything together. Bring the mixture up to the boil and then simmer it for about 20 minutes to allow it to thicken up a little. Season to taste before serving.

**Cook's note**
I use cannellini beans, which are the beans used in cans of baked beans, rather than the beans in their sweetened tomato sauce, but you could use them instead, especially if you want to make it for children.

# Chicken Casserole

On those mornings when I wake up to the sound of the rain pelting against the window as the wind howls outside, I want to pull my duvet up over my nose and never leave the bed rather than go outside and face the blustery day. When I do have to go out I find myself thinking about what comforting food I can cook for dinner when I get home. The thought of coming back and preparing meals like this one makes facing the elements seem not quite so bad.

**Serves 4**

1kg chicken legs and/or thighs, skin on
olive oil
1 onion, diced
1 carrot, diced
1 celery stick, diced
1 garlic clove, crushed
2 leeks, finely sliced (optional)
1 tablespoon plain flour
1 glass white wine
400ml chicken stock
a few sprigs of fresh thyme
2 bay leaves
sea salt and freshly ground black pepper

Preheat the oven to 160°C/ fan 140°C/gas mark 3.

Brown the chicken pieces in a little olive oil in a large flameproof casserole dish then remove it and set aside.

Add the onion, carrot, celery and garlic to the dish and sauté over a medium heat until the vegetables soften and the onion starts to turn translucent. Add the leeks (if using) and sauté the vegetables for a minute or so more.

Stir the flour into the vegetables then add the wine to the dish and turn the heat up so that the wine bubbles. Add the stock, thyme and bay leaves to the dish and season well.

Return the chicken to the dish and bring the casserole to the boil. Cover the dish with a lid and cook the casserole in the oven for 1 hour. Then remove the lid and cook it for a further 20–30 minutes, until the chicken is cooked through and falling off the bone. Skim off any excess fat and then check the seasoning before serving.

# Cheesy Mash

Say the words 'cheesy mash' to anyone and you're pretty much guaranteed a smile – piles of soft, fluffy mash with cheese and butter stirred through is pretty hard to resist.

**Serves 4**

1kg King Edward or Maris Piper
   potatoes
a splash of milk
50g butter
100g mature Cheddar cheese,
   grated
sea salt

Peel and cut the potatoes roughly into quarters, but making sure they are about the same size so that they cook at the same time. Add them to a large pan of salted water, bring it to the boil and cook the potatoes until tender.

Once the potatoes are cooked drain them completely so that there's no water left and leave them to stand for a few minutes to dry a little. Mash them until smooth and then stir in the milk, butter and cheese, which will melt in the heat of the potato as you stir it in. Season with a little sea salt before serving, if required.

**Cook's notes**
If you can, invest in a potato ricer. It will give you the very best, smooth and fluffy mash. I couldn't be without mine.

# Snow days

Even now, as an adult, I still get incredibly excited when I wake up to snowfall. The sight of everything covered in a blanket of white snow and snowflakes gently fluttering down like feathers from the sky is quite magical.

The outside world seems so enchanting; gardens and woods covered in snow take on a completely new character and seem to beckon you to explore them as the world we know becomes a Narnia-like fantasy.

Ten things to do when the snow is falling thick and heavy outside:

*Wrap up warm in your coat, scarf, hat and gloves, rush outside and sink your feet into the snow. Stand still and listen: isn't it quiet and muffled? Walk through the crisp, virgin snow listening to the crunch under your boots and looking back at the deep footprints you make. Look up to the sky at the softly falling snowflakes and feel them gently flutter onto your eyelashes and cheeks, and melt on your warm skin.*

*When the snow stops falling walk through a park and capture forever the beauty of the winter wonderland through the lens of your camera.*

*Call on friends and have a snowball fight or make snow angels.*

*Come in from the cold, pull off your wet things and change into warm, dry clothes. Make some hot chocolate and top it with whipped cream or fluffy marshmallows. Cup your hands around the mug and feel the warmth seep back into your hands as they slowly defrost, then sit by a hot radiator and wriggle your numb toes as you sip your chocolate.*

*Spend the day curled up with a crisp, new book or pick up a battered old favourite, and lose yourself in it.*

*Sit by the window snugly wrapped up in a blanket and watch the snow softly falling down whilst knitting or cross-stitching.*

*Make a large pot of thick, hearty soup and serve it with crusty bread, then bake biscuits and eat them warm from the oven.*

*Open a box of chocolates, sit back and watch an Audrey Hepburn film... or two.*

*Run a hot bath, full to the brim with scented bubbles, then sink into it and let it sooth you. Pamper yourself with body cream, put on a facemask and paint your toenails with glossy polish.*

*Make a snowman – of course!*

# Oxtail Broth

Oxtail has the most deliciously intense, beefy flavour that you wouldn't believe and the gelatine in the bone creates a wonderful broth full of heart and soul. It's especially good and nourishing if you're feeling in need of restoration.

**Serves 4**

olive oil
1kg oxtail, cut into pieces
1 onion, finely diced
1 carrot, finely diced
1 celery stick, finely diced
1 garlic clove, crushed
1.5 litres beef stock
a few sprigs of fresh thyme
100g button mushrooms, wiped
    clean
sea salt and freshly ground black
    pepper

Drizzle a little olive oil into a large pan and heat it over a high heat. Add the oxtail and brown it well on all sides then remove and set it aside.

Turn the heat down to medium and add the onion, carrot, celery and garlic. Sauté the vegetables for about 5 minutes until they start to soften.

Return the browned oxtail to the pan and add the rest of the ingredients. If the stock doesn't completely cover the oxtail top it up with water until it does. Bring the liquid to the boil then turn the heat right down so that the stock is barely simmering, with just the occasional bubble rising to the surface. Let the soup simmer like this for 3–4 hours, until the meat is meltingly tender, regularly skimming off the scum that rises to the surface.

Strain the soup through a fine sieve, ideally lined with muslin, and then skim off any excess fat and check the seasoning. To serve add a piece of oxtail to each bowl.

**Cook's note**
Despite the name, oxtail these days doesn't necessarily come from an ox; it can come from any beef cattle. The name is, however, reflective of the part of the animal it comes from: the tail. But don't let this put you off; it's incredibly tasty and meaty and if you didn't know what it was and you ate it off the bone you'd think it was no different to any other cut of beef, except perhaps more flavoursome. I urge you to try it.

# Beef and Ale Stew with Dumplings

When you've been out on a frosty winter's day, bright and sparkly but so bitingly cold you can see your breath, you need a good old fashioned stew to come home to; one that will warm you from the tip of your red nose to the tips of your frozen toes. And for this purpose you can't get much better than a beef and ale stew with dumplings.

**Serves 4–6**

olive oil
800g good stewing beef, such as shin of beef or chuck steak, cut into bite-sized chunks
2 onions, halved and sliced
2 garlic cloves, crushed
2 carrots, roughly chopped into bite-sized pieces
150g baby button mushrooms, wiped clean
1 tablespoon plain flour
330ml good strong ale
500ml beef stock
2 or 3 sprigs of fresh thyme
sea salt and freshly ground black pepper

**For the dumplings**
100g self-raising flour
50g suet
salt
thick crusty bread, to serve

Heat a flameproof casserole dish over a high heat and drizzle in a little olive oil. Season the beef with salt and pepper then add it to the dish and brown it well so that it forms a dark crust. Do this in batches so that you don't overcrowd the pan, as this will create steam, which prevents the beef from browning well. Remove the beef from the pan once it's browned.

Drizzle a little more olive oil into the dish and add the onions and garlic. Sauté them for a few minutes then add the carrots and the mushrooms and sauté the vegetables for about 5 minutes. Next add the flour and mix it well into the vegetables, then return the beef to the dish along with the ale, stock and thyme. Season with a little salt and lots of black pepper then bring the liquid up to the boil. Reduce the heat so that the liquid is just barely simmering and leave the stew to cook for 3–4 hours, until the beef is tender. If the liquid starts to reduce too much pop on a lid and add a little water if necessary. If it isn't reducing to your liking turn the heat up a little.

To make the dumplings place the flour, suet and a pinch of salt in a mixing bowl and stir in just enough cold water to form a soft dough. Flour your hands and form 8–12 even-sized small balls for the dumplings. To cook the dumplings, place them on top of the stew 30 minutes before the end of the cooking time and put a lid on the casserole dish.

Serve the stew with thick crusty bread.

**Cook's note**
When you're making a stew or casserole it's important to brown the meat very well over a high heat, so that it forms a dark crust. This means that the sugars in the meat are caramelising and this gives it an incredible flavour. The bottom of the casserole dish will turn brown and get bits stuck to it which is just what you want, as that's where all that flavour is. When you add the liquid to the dish scrape the bottom of it with a wooden spoon so that all the bits get mixed in with the liquid.

'Twas the night before Christmas, when all through the house, Not a creature was stirring, not even a mouse...

*The Night Before Christmas* Clement Clarke Moore

# Christmas...

If you're as old as you feel I'm about eleven years old and I'm gently tugging at the corners of the Christmas presents under the tree, so that I can steal a glimpse of what's inside, then turning them around to hide the evidence – that was the first and last year Mum put the presents under the tree before Christmas Eve night! And long before the big day I'm breaking off the peaks of icing on the Christmas cake and popping them into my mouth. It was all just too tempting and I was far too excited to wait. When it comes to Christmas that little girl is still alive inside of me and just as excited about the whole thing. But of course these days the excitement is more about the food than anything else.

Money was tight when we were growing up so, although we ate well, there was never an excess of food during the year, but at Christmas time we would eat like kings. Mum would save up for months and months, and buy bits and bobs – a box of biscuits here, a bottle of sherry there – each week to be saved for Christmas. In the days running up to it she'd bake mince pies and sausage rolls, and she'd cover the cake she'd baked with marzipan and icing peaked on top to look like snow. We weren't allowed to touch any of the food until Christmas Eve and then it all came out for a spectacular feast to gorge on over the whole of the Christmas period and beyond.

At the centre of the feast was the turkey. It was a big event when it was brought home and we would be wide-eyed when we saw the huge bird. We always had a much larger one than necessary for a family of four, to allow for lots of sandwiches and bowls of turkey stew in the days after the big lunch. It seemed to a little girl like me that that meat was never ending and I loved opening the fridge and pulling bits off the turkey – which is probably why I love having a chicken in the fridge now – or eating a plateful with pickled onions, sausage rolls and other delights while watching a film.

Now I get to stock up and cook festive meals and I love to plan it all. I like to sit down with a cup of tea and make a list of all the wonderful luxuries I'm going to stock up on and decide on meals to cook for family and friends over the festive period.

The cheeses are compulsory; a fat wedge of Brie and a slab of Stilton will suffice, but a block of good Cheddar is sometimes good for more variety. Sherry and port – my personal favourite – are the must-have evening tipples. I always buy a gammon joint, which I cook on Christmas Eve and then keep in the fridge, ready to be cut off in thick slices when we have guests or we're simply feeling peckish. And I often buy a rib of beef, which we'll sometimes have for our Christmas Eve dinner, with plenty left over for the coming days.

I look forward to the Boxing Day meal almost as much as the Christmas day lunch. A plateful of cold cuts of turkey, roast beef or gammon with coleslaw, pickled onions and perhaps some freshly roasted potatoes is simply glorious. And in the coming days the traditional turkey sandwich, made with thick, crusty bread and a dollop of mayonnaise, is the perfect snack. I never tire of Christmas leftovers; on the contrary, I revel in them.

I'm making a list,
I'm checking it twice ...

*Stilton, smoked salmon, brandy butter, clementines, double cream, cranberries, mince pies, Brussels sprouts, parsnips, streaky bacon, chestnuts*

I bought my last few presents in bustling Regent Street tonight, weaving in and out of crowds of people carrying bags and bags of presents, all wrapped up warm against the cold, cold foggy weather. Then I came home and wrapped the gifts I'd bought by the light of the christmas tree whilst drinking a glass of port.

*Blog entry, December 2006*

# Cashew Nut Brittle

This is good at any time but particularly at Christmas. Broken into shards and popped into little bags tied with ribbon, it makes lovely presents to pop under the tree ready to give to special friends.

I quite like to use the same amount of nuts to sugar so that the end result is more nut than brittle but if you prefer more brittle feel free to halve the amount of nuts.

The combination of salt and caramel is, perhaps surprisingly, quite delicious but if you prefer you can use regular, plain cashew nuts instead. Take care when making caramel and check the golden rules on page 111.

300g caster sugar
150–300g salted cashew nuts

Line a baking tray with baking parchment for cooling the nut brittle on – this will stop it sticking to the tray and you'll be able to simply peel off the baking parchment once it's cool.

Heat a medium, heavy-based pan over a medium heat and add the sugar to the pan, so that it's evenly distributed. After a while the sugar will start to dissolve and turn golden. Shake it every now and then so that it dissolves evenly. Be patient and don't be tempted to turn the heat up too high as the caramel can quickly get too hot, taking on a bitter, burnt taste, and be difficult to cool down. Once the sugar has completely dissolved and turned a deep, golden, caramel colour add the nuts to the pan and swirl it around so that they get covered in the caramel. You may find it helpful to use a wooden spoon to help turn the nuts in the caramel so that they get completely covered.

Quickly and carefully turn the caramel-covered nuts onto the lined baking tray and allow them to cool completely. The brittle will set quite quickly but will take about an hour to cool completely.

Once the nut brittle is cool you can break it up – a small hammer will help with this!

# Christmas Cookies

I absolutely love these cookies; they're so delicious I could quite happily eat a plateful all on my own. They capture all those sweet flavours that remind me of Christmas – orange, cinnamon, sultanas, nuts – and I'd be very happy to wake up to them in my stocking on Christmas morning. I'm quite sure too, that Father Christmas would be happy to find them waiting for him, along with a glass of milk or perhaps a small sherry, when he comes down the chimney.

**Makes approximately 30 cookies**

125g butter
150g golden caster sugar
1 egg
150g plain flour
1 teaspoon baking powder
zest of 1 orange
$\frac{1}{2}$ teaspoon ground cinnamon
80g sultanas
50g walnuts, roughly chopped
50g brazil nuts, roughly chopped

Preheat the oven to 180°C/ fan 160°C/gas mark 4. Line a baking tray with baking parchment.

Place the butter and sugar together in a medium mixing bowl and cream them together until the mixture is light and fluffy. Add the egg, flour, baking powder, orange zest and cinnamon to the bowl and mix everything together well. Finally mix in the sultanas and nuts.

Dollop heaped teaspoon-sized balls of cookie mixture on to the lined baking tray – you will need to cook them in batches. It will look like a measly amount but trust me, they will spread and get bigger as they cook, so make sure they're well spaced apart on the tray.

Bake the cookies for about 10 minutes until they're lightly golden then transfer them onto a wire rack to cool. They'll be very soft when they come out of the oven but don't worry; they'll firm up as they cool.

# Chestnut and Smoky Bacon Soup

I love those little bags of chestnuts sold from drums where they're roasting over hot coals. Peeling too-hot chestnuts with too-cold fingers on a frosty day is quite joyous. But when it comes to cooking I find them far too fiddly and I lack patience. So over the Christmas period I keep vacuum packs of cooked chestnuts for stuffing and for this, my favourite seasonal soup.

**Serves 6**

a knob of butter
200g smoked back bacon, rind removed and roughly chopped
1 onion, diced
400g vacuum packed chestnuts, (or freshly roasted and shelled, if you prefer)
800ml chicken stock
sea salt and freshly ground black pepper
double cream, to garnish (optional)
crusty bread, to serve

Melt the butter in a large pan over a medium heat. Add the chopped bacon to the pan then sauté it until well coloured, but don't allow it to turn crispy. Remove the bacon from the pan with a slotted spoon, leaving behind the fat, then add the onion to the pan and sauté until it softens. At this stage return the bacon to the pan along with the chestnuts and chicken stock, and bring the mixture to the boil.

Simmer the soup for 5 minutes then remove it from the heat and blend it until smooth, adding a little water if it's too thick for your liking. Season the soup to taste before ladling it into bowls. If you're feeling decadent, add a retro swirl of double cream and serve with crusty bread.

*Chestnuts roasting on an open fire,*
*Jack Frost nipping at your nose,*
*Yuletide carols being sung by a choir,*
*And folks dressed up like Eskimos*

'The Christmas Song'
Mel Tormé and Robert Wells

It was chilly and dark outside as I sat writing christmas cards last night. I was drinking spicy, orangey, brandy-laced hot chocolate to warm me through. Chocolate melted into warm milk with a splash of brandy and a drizzle of honey.

*Blog entry, December 2006*

# A Recipe to Evoke the Spirit of Christmas

Sometimes you need a little time out to stop the world for a moment, make everything still and just be. In times such as these that you need a reminder of what Christmas is all about. This very special recipe will help to bring back a little of the magic.

Serves 1

warm pyjamas
fluffy bed socks
1 mug full of milk, preferably
full fat
1 slab of 70% cocoa solids dark
chocolate, about 25g for the hot
chocolate, the rest to eat
1 cinnamon stick
a dash of brandy, rum or orange
liqueur such as Cointreau
(optional)
sugar or honey, to taste
a little whipped double cream to
top the hot chocolate with
(optional)
a Christmas film such as
*A Christmas Carol* or
*It's a Wonderful Life*
a cosy blanket

Start by pulling on your pyjamas and bed socks, and then pad to the kitchen. Pour the milk into a pan and slowly heat it up. As the milk starts to heat add squares of the chocolate to taste, the cinnamon stick and a generous dash of your favourite tipple.

When the chocolate has melted and the milk has heated through pour the hot chocolate into a mug. Add a little sugar or honey and whisk everything together. Top with whipped double cream for a real treat.

Finally, put the film on, wrap yourself in a blanket and curl up on the sofa with the hot chocolate.

*The crisp leaves of holly, mistletoe, and ivy reflected back the light, as if so many little mirrors had been scattered there; and such a mighty blaze went roaring up the chimney, as that dull petrifaction of a hearth had never known in Scrooge's time, or Marley's, or for many and many a winter season gone. Heaped up on the floor, to form a kind of throne, were turkeys, geese, game, poultry, brawn, great joints of meat, sucking-pigs, long wreaths of sausages, mince-pies, plum-puddings, barrels of oysters, red-hot chestnuts, cherry-cheeked apples, juicy oranges, luscious pears, immense twelfth-cakes, and seething bowls of punch, that made the chamber dim with their delicious steam.*

*A Christmas Carol Charles Dickens*

# Port-glazed Gammon

I love Christmas Eve. It always seemed so magical to me when I was a child and thankfully a little of that magic has stayed with me. I love the last-minute wrapping of presents, the preparations around the house, and of course the cooking and the baking. I love the evening the most, when it's dark outside and the lights of the Christmas tree are twinkling and I can sit back with a glass of something merry, curled up with Rob, and watch a Christmassy film.

I always cook a gammon on Christmas Eve, to see us over the Christmas period, and to me the smell of it cooking with vegetables, peppercorns and a bay leaf – just like the smell of giblet stock slowly simmering and the turkey roasting in the oven – is the smell of Christmas.

I usually serve the gammon cold but will sometimes serve it hot and let the rest cool down for another meal. My favourite way to serve it is cold with Roast Potatoes (see page 152) or Roasted Potato Wedges (see page 104) and The Parsons Family Coleslaw (see page 72).

**Approximately 12 servings**

1 unsmoked gammon, approximately 2kg
1 onion, quartered
1 celery stick, roughly chopped
1 carrot, roughly chopped
8 black peppercorns
1 bay leaf

**For the glaze**
100ml port
2 tablespoons caster sugar

Put the gammon into a large pan and cover it with water then add the vegetables, peppercorns and bay leaf. Bring the water to the boil then simmer the gammon for 20 minutes per 500g. After this time check that the gammon is cooked through by inserting a skewer into the middle and making sure the juices run clear.

Preheat the oven to 220°C/ fan 200°C/gas mark 7. Line a baking tray with baking parchment.

Cut the skin and fat off the gammon and then put it onto the lined tray. It is important to line the tray as the glaze is very sticky and will easily burn on the tray, making it hard to clean.

Place the port and sugar in a small pan and boil them together until the mixture turns syrupy and reduces by about two thirds, then spoon or brush it with a pastry brush all over the gammon.

Bake the gammon for about 15 minutes, spooning the glaze over the gammon once or twice as it cooks, until it's nicely glazed.

**Cook's note**
Gammon can sometimes be very salty and need soaking before it's cooked. To check, cut a little piece off and fry it until cooked through then taste it. If it is salty soak it overnight or all day in cold water, changing the water a few times. Alternatively put it into a pan, cover it with water and bring it to the boil then drain away the water before cooking it.

# Christmas Morning Breakfast

On Christmas morning I wake early with a bubbling feeling of excitement inside of me. I lean over in bed to see if Rob's awake yet (please let him be!), kiss him and wish him a happy Christmas, and then go downstairs and into the living room. I turn on the Christmas tree lights and then go to the window and look out. Who's up? Which lights are on in the houses down the street? I get an almost magical feeling, thinking of all the people in their houses waking up, preparing turkeys and exchanging gifts, knowing that it's quiet on the roads and deserted in the streets. The outside world seems silent and peaceful on Christmas morning, and that sense of peace, and of hope, stays with me throughout the day.

I walk to the kitchen and switch on the kettle, and then I set about making my traditional Christmas morning breakfast. I make it just for me, as Rob insists on nothing but toast and a cup of tea. It seems almost too decadent for breakfast for one, but I love it so and it is, after all, Christmas. It's become one of my own little traditions, a breakfast which I save only for Christmas, and so it is that on this one day of the year I scramble eggs, tumble them onto a plate, lay thin slices of Scottish smoked salmon over them, and then pour a solitary glass of Bucks fizz, clink my glass against the side of Rob's mug of tea, and drink a toast to a very happy Christmas.

**Serves 1**

2–3 eggs
a dash of double cream
    (optional)
a knob of butter
1 or 2 slices of smoked salmon,
    torn into strips
sea salt and freshly ground
    black pepper
hot, buttered toast, to serve
    (optional)

**For the Bucks fizz**
fresh orange juice
Champagne

Lightly beat the eggs with the salt, pepper and cream, if using, to combine them.

Heat the butter over a medium heat in a non-stick saucepan and when it starts to gently sizzle add in the eggs and stir them continuously. The instant they start to come together take the pan off the heat and pile the eggs onto a plate then lay over the ribbons of smoked salmon. If you like you can serve it with a slice of hot buttered toast.

For the Bucks fizz, pour a little fresh orange juice into a glass and top it up with Champagne (about one third orange juice to two thirds Champagne).

# Turkey and Cranberry Parcels

These little parcels are quite delicious and are great for using up leftover turkey. The crispy, flaky filo pastry gives way to reveal and unctuous, gooey turkey filling with sweet, plump cranberries and a mild cheese taste. With thanks to my friend Vanessa for the inspiration.

**Serves 2 as a main course or 4 as a starter**

olive oil
2 shallots, finely diced
400g cooked turkey, cut into bite-
    sized pieces
100ml double cream
a handful of mature Cheddar
    cheese
2 handfuls of plump, dried
    cranberries
270g packet (12 sheets) filo pastry
70g butter, melted
sea salt and freshly ground black
    pepper
winter salad leaves, to serve

Preheat the oven to 200°C/ fan 180°C/gas mark 6. Line a baking tray with baking parchment.

Heat a little olive oil in a large non-stick frying pan over a medium heat. Add the shallots to the pan and sauté them for a few minutes then add the turkey, cream, cheese and cranberries. Season the mixture well and simmer it, stirring, until it turns thick and gooey then turn off the heat.

Lay out a sheet of filo pastry and brush it with a little of the melted butter then lay a second sheet on top and brush that with a little butter. Top with a third sheet of pastry and brush it with butter too, then put a quarter of the turkey mixture into the centre of the pastry. Pull up the edges of the pastry into the centre and press them together to form a round, sealed parcel. Repeat with the remaining pastry and filling to make another 3 parcels.

Carefully place the parcels onto the lined baking tray then brush the remaining butter over. Cook the parcels for about 20 minutes, until golden brown.

Serve the parcels hot or cold with some winter salad leaves.

# Roast Goose with Chestnut and Pancetta Stuffing

Although turkey is my traditional Christmas lunch I love the nostalgic notion of the Victorian Christmas roast goose from the Dickens novels. If I'm serving six or more people with one goose, I like to roast a chicken as well and pile the meat onto separate platters to bump up the offering, as geese tend to be more cavity than meat. Cabbage, particularly Savoy or red cabbage, is good to serve with goose and it would be a crime not to roast potatoes in all that delicious fat that's released from the goose as it cooks.

**Serves 6**

**For the goose giblet stock**
giblets from the goose
1 onion, halved
1 stick of celery, roughly chopped
1 carrot, roughly chopped
1 bay leaf
8 peppercorns

**For the chestnut and pancetta stuffing**
100g pancetta, roughly chopped
1 onion, finely chopped
200g vacuum packed chestnuts
8 pork sausages, approximately 450g, skinned
2 sprigs of fresh thyme
freshly ground black pepper

**For the goose**
1 onion, quartered
2 carrots, roughly chopped
2 celery sticks, roughly chopped
1 goose, approximately 6kg
sea salt and freshly ground black pepper

First make the giblet stock. Wash the giblets and put them into a pan and cover with water. Add the rest of the ingredients and bring the water up to the boil. Simmer for $1\frac{1}{2}$ hours, skimming off any scum that rises to the surface as it cooks. Sieve the simmered stock into a clean pan. Increase the heat and allow the stock to reduce until happy with the flavour. Set aside to use for the gravy.

Meanwhile, to make the stuffing, sauté the pancetta in a small non-stick frying pan until it is cooked through (you won't need any oil as the pancetta will release its own fat). Remove the pancetta from the pan with a slotted spoon, leaving the fat behind, and then add the chopped onion to the pan. Sauté the onion until softened and then put it into a bowl with the pancetta, chestnuts and sausagemeat. Add the leaves from the sprigs of thyme and season the mixture with black pepper then mix it all together well with your hands.

Put the vegetables for the goose into a large roasting tin. Preheat the oven to 220°C/fan 200°C/gas mark 7.

Prick the goose all over with a fork to help release the fat during cooking. Remove any excess white fat, particularly around the opening of the cavity. Wrap the legs in foil to protect them from the heat.

Stuff the neck of the goose with as much of the stuffing as you can and secure it with a metal skewer then roll the rest into balls and put them into the cavity. Season the goose with salt and pepper and then lay it on the bed of vegetables in the roasting tin.

Roast the goose for 30 minutes, and then reduce the oven temperature to 180°C/fan 160°C/gas mark 4 and cook it for a further $1\frac{3}{4}$–$2\frac{1}{2}$ hours, until the juices run clear when the thickest part of the legs are pierced with a skewer. Every now and then carefully pour out the excess fat that forms in the roasting tin and lift and tip the goose vertically to allow the juices that accumulate inside the cavity to run out.

Once cooked, leave the goose to rest for at least 20 minutes, wrapped up in foil then covered with a tea towel to keep it warm.

While the goose is resting, make the Gravy (see page 154) using the giblet stock and the vegetables in the roasting tray.

The goose looks quite splendid laid out in all its glory on a platter but I find it easier to carve it in the kitchen so I tend to ceremoniously show it to my guests and then take it away again to carve it. I carve the meat off the breasts in slices and then pull off the legs and roughly cut or pull off all the meat from them. I then pile all of the meat back onto the platter. If I'm serving chicken meat too I pile that onto a separate platter and take them both to the table with the gravy for a wonderful feast.

**Cook's note**
The Chestnut and pancetta stuffing is also very good served with chicken or game birds.

# Christmas Pudding Cheesecakes

I'm not a huge lover of Christmas pudding and tend to have just a little for Christmas lunch. I therefore usually have some leftover. These cheesecakes, which are in fact a modified version of the ones on page 108, are the perfect way of using up the leftovers, and they're really rather fabulous.

**Makes 4 individual cheesecakes**

**For the base**
75g digestive biscuits
25g butter, melted

**For the topping**
200g cream cheese
$\frac{1}{2}$ teaspoon vanilla extract
icing sugar, to taste
150g cooked cold Christmas
    pudding, crumbled

You can make the cheesecakes in ramekins or using metal ring moulds. If you're using ramekins, line them completely with foil, letting it over extend the top so you can easily pull the cheesecakes out.

Crush the biscuits until they form even-sized crumbs. Place the butter in a medium pan and heat it gently until melted. Stir the crumbs into the melted butter. Place the metal rings or ramekins onto serving plates then press a quarter of the biscuit mixture into each. Set aside to cool.

Place the cream cheese and vanilla extract in a medium bowl and mix them together until smooth. Add a tablespoon of icing sugar at a time, mixing well, until the topping is

sweet enough for your taste. Then stir in the crumbled Christmas pudding. Spoon the mixture over the bases in the rings or ramekins and smooth over the tops. Chill in the fridge for at least 4 hours.

When the cheesecakes are set and you are ready to serve them, if you've used ramekins simply pull the foil to lift the cheesecakes out and place them on a serving plate. If you've used metal rings use a blowtorch to heat the moulds a little, to make them easier to slide off or, if you haven't got a blowtorch, wrap a hot cloth around them for a minute.

# Christmas Trifle

No matter how much you eat at Christmas time, you can always find room for trifle; it simply isn't Christmas without one!

**Serves 6**

1 raspberry jam-filled Swiss roll
50–100ml Madeira or sherry
300g fruit, such as frozen
    raspberries, thawed, mandarin
    segments or fruits seeped in
    alcohol

500ml Home-made (see page 166) or
    ready-made fresh chilled custard
300ml double cream, lightly
    whipped
70% cocoa solids dark chocolate,
    to decorate

Slice the Swiss roll into rounds and line a trifle bowl with them. Lay them against the sides of the glass so that they look pretty from the outside and put one slice in the middle at the bottom of the bowl. Drizzle over a

little of the Madeira or sherry and set aside to allow the sponge to soak it up. Continue to drizzle the alcohol over until it is all used up or the sponge can take no more.

Tumble the fruit over the Swiss roll and then dollop over the custard. Top the trifle with whipped cream and finally grate over some dark chocolate.

# Christmas Pudding and Chocolate Pancakes

This is another great recipe for using up Christmas pudding. The crumbled Christmas pudding melded with liquid chocolate and wrapped in pancakes is rich, dark and quite divine.

**Makes 4 pancakes**

**For the pancakes**
60g plain flour
1 egg
150ml milk
vegetable oil, for cooking

**For the filling**
50g 70% cocoa solids dark
    chocolate
250g cooked cold Christmas
    pudding, crumbled
whipped cream, brandy butter or
    vanilla ice cream, to serve

Sift the flour into a bowl and make a well in the centre, then crack the egg into it. Whisk the egg, gradually incorporating the flour until it starts to form a paste and then slowly whisk in the milk so that you get a smooth mixture the consistency of single cream. Leave the batter to stand for 30 minutes.

Preheat the oven to 200°C/fan 180°C/ gas mark 6.

To melt the chocolate, fill a small pan about a quarter full with water and bring it to the boil. Break the chocolate into pieces and place it in a small heatproof bowl. Put the bowl over the pan of water, making sure the base doesn't touch the water. Reduce the temperature so the water is just simmering and the steam will gently melt the chocolate. Stir the crumbled Christmas pudding into the melted chocolate. Set it aside while you make the pancakes.

To make the pancakes brush a little oil onto the base of an 18–20cm frying pan using a pastry brush. Heat the pan over a high heat so that it's nice and hot and then turn the heat down to medium. Add a ladleful of batter to the pan and swirl it around so that it covers the bottom of the pan. Cook for a minute or two until the bottom of the pancake starts to turn golden. You can check this by loosening the edges with a palette knife and checking underneath. When the bottom of the pancake is cooked flip it over with the palette knife or by tossing it in the air. The other side won't take as long to cook, only about 30–60 seconds.

When the pancake is cooked transfer it to a plate. Spoon a quarter of the Christmas pudding and chocolate mixture into the middle of the pancake and roll it up.

Repeat to make the remaining pancakes, brushing a little more oil onto the bottom of the frying pan each time to prevent the pancakes from sticking.

When all the pancakes are cooked and filled, put them onto a baking tray and bake in the oven for 8–10 minutes to warm them through. Serve with a dollop of whipped cream, some brandy butter or a scoop of vanilla ice cream.

# Christmas Pavlova

This very festive Pavlova is wonderful to serve at any time over the Christmas period and is guaranteed to make your family and friends' eyes light up in delight!

**Serves 8–10**

**For the base**
4 egg whites
220g caster sugar
1 teaspoon white wine vinegar

**For the topping**
400ml double cream, lightly whipped
4 clementines, peeled and
  segmented
40g dark chocolate, such as Green
  & Black's Maya Gold chocolate

Preheat the oven to 140°C/
fan 120°C/gas mark 1.

Whisk the eggs until they form stiff peaks and you can hold the bowl upside down without them falling out – I know this can be quite worrying the first few times you do this but they really won't fall out if they're whisked enough, I promise! Next add the sugar one tablespoon at a time, whisking each tablespoon in before adding the next. Once all the sugar has been incorporated and dissolved the mixture should be firm and glossy, and not feel gritty – test this by taking a pinch of the mixture and rubbing it between your finger and thumb. Finally whisk in the white wine vinegar.

Dot a little of the mixture into each corner of a sheet of baking parchment then turn it over and stick it onto a large baking tray. You may find it helpful to first draw a circle on the parchment, approximately 24cm in diameter, to guide you when shaping the meringue. If you do, make sure you turn the paper over so that the pencil markings are face down on the tray. Dollop the mixture onto the paper and spread it out with a spatula to make a circular shape, flattened in the middle and raised a little around the edges.

Bake the meringue in the oven for 1 hour, then turn the oven off and leave the meringue inside to dry out for several hours, until the oven is completely cool – ideally overnight.

To assemble the Pavlova, spread the cream over the meringue and then lay the clementine segments in a decorative pattern on top.

To melt the chocolate, fill a small pan about a quarter full with water and bring it to the boil. Break the chocolate into pieces and place it in a small heatproof bowl. Put the bowl over the pan of water, making sure the base doesn't touch the water. Reduce the temperature so the water is just simmering and the steam will gently melt the chocolate. Drizzle the melted chocolate over the Pavlova just before serving.

**Cook's note**
Green & Black's Maya Gold chocolate, laced with orange and spices, really makes this Pavlova very special and festive but if you can't get hold of it use any 70% cocoa solids dark chocolate, ideally one with spices in it, such as chilli.

# a

**apples**
Apple and raspberry tart *41*
Baked apples *167*
Red apple and Parma ham salad *37*
Toffee apples *139*

**asparagus**
Asparagus, avocado and pea shoot
 salad *14*
Asparagus, courgette and lemon pasta *25*
Baked Camembert with asparagus
 dippers *23*

Autumnal chicken *125*

**avocado**
Asparagus, avocado and pea shoot
 salad *14*
Chicken and avocado salad *34*
Parma ham-wrapped avocado slices *96*
Summer salad *53*

# b

**bacon**
Bean and bacon soup *177*
Brie and bacon sandwich *127*
Chestnut and smoky bacon soup *189*
Full English breakfast *146*
Warm bacon and scallop salad *86*

Baked apples *167*
Baked Camembert with asparagus
 dippers *23*
Baked potatoes *137*
Baked pumpkins *136*
Baked sea bass with spinach and
 sautéed potatoes *77*
Baked sweet potato *126*
banana pancakes, Honey and *169*
basil soup, Chilled cherry tomato and *50*
Bean and bacon soup *177*

**beef**
Beef and ale stew with dumplings *183*
Beef burgers *67*
Pot roast beef brisket *155*
Roast beef salad *35*
Roast rib of beef *151*
Spaghetti Bolognese *161*
Steak and goat's cheese salad *22*
Steak, Camembert and mushroom
 pancakes *101*

**biscuits**
Christmas cookies *188*
Cinnamon hearts *28*
Halloween biscuits *135*

blackberry and chocolate tart, Pear,
 *129*
*...blackberry picking with my mum
 and my sister; lying on freshly cut
 grass making daisy chains... 31*

**blueberries**
Blueberry cheesecakes *108*
Midsummer cake *56*
Summer pavlova *43*
Watermelon, blueberry and mint salad *55*

**bread**
Brie and bacon sandwich *127*
Cheesy garlic bread *97*
Eggy bread *126*
Fried duck eggs on toast *19*
Sausage baguettes with caramelised
 onions *137*

Brie and bacon sandwich *127*
brittle, Cashew nut *186*
broth, Oxtail *181*
burgers, Beef *67*
burgers, Lamb *67*

# c

**cabbage**
Chorizo and Savoy cabbage risotto *172*
Warm duck and red cabbage salad *174*

**cake**
Blueberry cheesecakes *108*
Duck egg chocolate cake *20*
Fairy cakes *142*
Midsummer cake *56*

Caramelised orange puffs *110*
Carrot and swede mash *155*
Cashew nut brittle *186*

**casseroles**
Chicken casserole *178*
Sausage and lentil casserole *175*

**cheese**
Brie and bacon sandwich *127*
Camembert and mushroom pancakes,
 Steak, *101*
Camembert with asparagus dippers,
 Baked *23*
Cheeseboard, The *116*
cheesecakes, Blueberry *108*
cheesecakes, Christmas pudding *198*
Cheese sauce for vegetables *106*
Cheese-smothered new potatoes *16*
Cheddar soup, English *121*
Cheese straws *98*
Cheesy garlic bread *97*
Cheesy mash *179*

cream cheese and cress wraps, Smoked
 salmon, *61*
Feta cheese and watercress sauce *13*
feta cheese, Roasted pumpkin and
 sweet potato with *132*
goat's cheese salad, Steak and *22*
halloumi and cherry tomato skewers,
 Chicken, *70*
parmesan cheese, Spaghetti with butter
 and *127*
Parmesan crusts, Pea-stuffed chicken
 breasts with *39*
Stichelton salad, Pear, fig and *103*

Cherry pie *44*
Cherry tomato and mint salsa *52*
Chestnut and smoky bacon soup *189*
chestnut and pancetta stuffing, Roast
 goose with *194*
chestnuts and mushrooms, Pot roast
 pheasants with *130*

**chicken**
Autumnal chicken *125*
Chicken and avocado salad *34*
Chicken casserole *178*
Chicken, halloumi and
 cherry tomato
 skewers *70*
Chicken in lemon and
 white wine *107*
Chicken stock or broth
 *156*
Heavenly roast
 chicken *148*
Lemon, chicken and
 spring onion salad
 *34*
Pea-stuffed chicken
 breasts with Parmesan crusts
 *39*
Pot roast chicken *123*

Chilled cherry tomato and basil soup *50*
chive omelette, Duck egg and *17*
chive potato salad, Warm *73*

**chocolate**
Chocolate orange ice cream *91*
Christmas pudding and chocolate
 pancakes *199*
Duck egg chocolate cake *20*
Eton mess *53*
Last summer fling crumble *47*
Marshmallow and chocolate chip ice
 cream *91*
Pear, blackberry and chocolate tart *129*
Strawberry chocolate meringues *112*

**chorizo**
Chorizo and new potato salad *38*
Chorizo and Savoy cabbage risotto *172*
Chorizo and tomato tart *64*

Christmas cookies 188
Christmas morning breakfast 192
Christmas pavlova 197
Christmas pudding and chocolate
    pancakes 199
Christmas pudding cheesecakes 198
Christmas trifle 198
Cinnamon hearts 28
coleslaw, The Parsons family 72

**courgettes**
Asparagus, courgette and lemon pasta 25
Vegetable skewers 70

crab parcels, Filo 84

**cream**
Asparagus, courgette and lemon
    pasta 25
clotted cream ice cream, Strawberry
    and 92
Creamy sausage pasta 122
Eton mess 53
Midsummer cake 56
Peaches and cream trifle 42
soured cream, Tomato and pasta soup
    with 125
Tipsy raspberries and cream 42

Creamy potato salad 73
Creamy sausage pasta 122
cress wraps, Smoked salmon, cream
    cheese and 61
Crispy and fluffy roast potatoes 152

**crumbles**
Last summer fling crumble 47
Plum crumble 165
Rhubarb crumble 27
...curling up on the sofa when it's dark
    and cold outside, watching
    fireworks light up the sky on Bonfire
    Night... 119

## d

**desserts**
Apple and raspberry tart 41
Baked apples 167
Blueberry cheesecakes 108
Caramelised orange puffs 110
Cherry pie 44
Christmas pavlova 197
Christmas pudding and chocolate
    pancakes 199
Christmas pudding cheesecakes 198
Christmas trifle 198
Eton mess 53
Home-made custard 166
Honey peaches 114
Last summer fling crumble 47

Orange and rhubarb jellies 26
Peaches and cream trifle 42
Pear, blackberry and chocolate tart 129
Plum crumble 165
Pomegranate and passion fruit jellies 113
Rhubarb crumble 27
Rosé wine and strawberry jellies 114
Summer pavlova 43
Strawberries with white balsamic
    vinegar 65
Strawberry chocolate meringues 112
Tipsy raspberries and cream 42

**duck**
duck and red cabbage salad, Warm 174
Duck egg and chive omelette 17
Duck egg chocolate cake 20
duck eggs on toast, Fried 19
duck eggs, Softly scrambled 19
dumplings, Beef and ale stew with 183

## e

**eggs**
Christmas morning breakfast 192
Christmas pavlova 197
Duck egg and chive omelette 17
Duck egg chocolate cake 20
Eggy bread 126
Eton mess 53
Fried duck eggs on toast 19
Home-made custard 166
Leek omelette 176
Scotch eggs 62
Softly scrambled duck eggs 19
Strawberry chocolate meringues 112
Summer pavlova 43

English Cheddar soup 121
Eton mess 53

## f

Fairy cakes 142
Feta cheese and watercress sauce 13
fig and Stichelton salad, Pear 103
Filo crab parcels 84

**fish**
Christmas morning breakfast 192
Fish pie 82
Poached salmon with watercress and
    chargrilled cherry tomatoes 83
sea bass with spinach and sautéed
    potatoes, Baked 77
Smoked salmon, cream cheese and
    cress wraps 61

...flowers in full bloom peeking out
    from beneath cotton wool snow... 23

Fried duck eggs on toast 19
Full English breakfast 146

## g

gammon, Port-glazed 191
garlic bread, Cheesy 97
Gravy 154
Green bean and herb rice 35

## h

Halloween biscuits 135

**ham**
Red apple and Parma ham salad 37
Summer salad 53

Heavenly roast chicken 148
Home-made custard 166
Home-made lemonade 32
Honey and banana pancakes 169
Honey peaches 114

## *index*

**ice cream**
Chocolate orange ice cream 91
Marshmallow and chocolate chip ice
    cream 91
Strawberry and clotted cream ice cream
    92
Summer berry ice cream 91
Vanilla ice cream 91

Iced orange wedges 58
...Idly running your fingertips over the
    grass whilst looking up at a blue,
    cloudless sky... 49

# j

**jelly**
Orange and rhubarb jellies *26*
Pomegranate and passion fruit jellies *113*
Rosé wine and strawberry jellies *114*

Jersey Royal salad *16*

# k

King prawn linguine *78*

# l

**lamb**
Lamb burgers *67*
Lamb shanks braised in red wine *100*
Shepherd's pie *163*
Slow lamb *160*

Leek omelette *176*
lemon and white wine, Chicken in *107*
lemon pasta, Asparagus, courgette and *25*
Lemon, chicken and spring onion salad *34*
lemonade, Home-made *32*
lentil casserole, Sausage and *175*
Lobster *88*

# m

Marinated black olives *96*
Marshmallow and chocolate chip ice cream *91*

**meat**
bacon and scallop salad, Warm *86*
bacon sandwich, Brie and *127*
bacon soup, Bean and *177*
bacon soup, Chestnut and smoky *189*
Beef and ale stew with dumplings *183*
beef brisket, Pot roast *155*
Beef burgers *67*
beef, Roast rib of *151*
beef salad, Roast *35*
Chicken and avocado salad *34*
chicken and spring onion salad, Lemon, *34*
chicken, Autumnal *125*
chicken breasts with Parmesan crusts, Pea-stuffed *39*
Chicken casserole *178*
Chicken, halloumi and cherry tomato skewers *70*
chicken, Heavenly roast *148*
Chicken in lemon and white wine *107*
chicken, Pot roast *123*

Chicken stock or broth *156*
Chorizo and new potato salad *38*
Chorizo and Savoy cabbage risotto *172*
Chorizo and tomato tart *64*
duck and red cabbage salad, Warm *174*
Full English breakfast *146*
gammon, Port-glazed *191*
goose with chestnut and pancetta stuffing, Roast *194*
Lamb shanks braised in red wine *100*
Oxtail broth *181*
Parma ham salad, Red apple and *37*
Parma ham-wrapped avocado slices *96*
pheasants with chestnuts and mushrooms, Pot roast *130*

pork, Slow roasted belly of *158*
Sausage and lentil casserole *175*
Sausage baguettes with caramelised onions *137*
Sausage and sweet potato mash *120*
sausage pasta, Creamy *122*
Scotch eggs *62*
Shepherd's pie *163*
Spaghetti Bolognese *161*
Steak and goat's cheese salad *22*
Steak, Camembert and mushroom pancakes *101*
Summer salad *53*
Toad in the hole *162*
Turkey and cranberry parcels *193*

**meringues**
Christmas pavlova *197*
Strawberry chocolate meringues *112*
Summer pavlova *43*

Midsummer cake *56*
mint salad, Watermelon, blueberry and *55*
mint salsa, Cherry tomato and *52*
mint sorbet, Raspberry and *92*

**mushrooms**
Pot roast pheasants with chestnuts and mushrooms *130*
Steak, Camembert and mushroom pancakes *101*

**mussels**
Mussels in white wine *81*
Mussels with saffron and capellini *79*

# o

olives, Marinated black *96*
omelette, Duck egg and chive *17*
omelette, Leek *176*

**onions**
caramelised onions, Sausage baguettes with *137*
spring onion salad, Lemon, chicken and *34*
Vegetable skewers *70*

**oranges**
Caramelised orange puffs *110*
Chocolate orange ice cream *91*
Iced orange wedges *58*
Orange and rhubarb jellies *26*

Oxtail broth *181*

# p

**pancakes**
Christmas pudding and chocolate pancakes *199*
Honey and banana pancakes *169*
Steak, Camembert and mushroom Pancakes *101*

pancetta stuffing, Roast goose with chestnut and *194*
Parma ham salad, Red apple and *37*
Parma ham-wrapped avocado slices *96*
passion fruit jellies, Pomegranate and *113*

**pasta**
Asparagus, courgette and lemon pasta *25*
capellini, Mussels with saffron and *79*
Creamy sausage pasta *122*
linguine, King prawn *78*
Spaghetti Bolognese *161*
Spaghetti with butter and parmesan cheese *127*
Tomato and pasta soup with soured cream *125*

**pastry**
Apple and raspberry tart *41*
Caramelised orange puffs *110*
Cheese straws *98*
Cherry pie *44*
Chorizo and tomato tart *64*
Filo crab parcels *84*
Turkey and cranberry parcels *193*

pavlova, Christmas *197*
pavlova, Summer *43*

**peaches**
Honey peaches *114*
Peaches and cream trifle *42*

**pears**
Pear, blackberry and chocolate tart *129*
Pear, fig and Stichelton salad *103*

pea shoot salad, Asparagus, avocado
and *14*

**peas**
Pea-stuffed chicken breasts with
Parmesan crusts *39*
Spring vegetable soup *12*

pheasants with chestnuts and
mushrooms, Pot roast *130*

**pies**
Cherry pie *44*
Fish pie *82*
Shepherd's pie *163*

Pimms and lemonade *58*
Plum crumble *165*
Poached salmon with watercress and
chargrilled cherry tomatoes *83*
Pomegranate and passion fruit
jellies *113*

**pork**
Port-glazed gammon *191*
Scotch eggs *62*
Slow roasted belly of pork *158*

Port-glazed gammon *191*

**potatoes**
Baked potatoes *137*
Baked sea bass with spinach and
sautéed potatoes *77*
Baked sweet potato *126*
Cheese-smothered new potatoes *16*
Cheesy mash *179*
Chorizo and new potato salad *38*
Creamy potato salad *73*
Crispy and fluffy roast potatoes *152*
Fish pie *82*
Jersey Royal salad *16*
Roasted potato wedges *104*
Shepherd's pie *163*
sweet potato mash, Sausage and *120*
prawn linguine, King *78*
sweet potato with feta cheese, Roasted
pumpkin and *132*
Warm chive potato salad *73*

Pot roast beef brisket *155*
Pot roast chicken *123*
Pot roast pheasants with chestnuts and
mushrooms *130*
prawn linguine, King *78*

puddings, Yorkshire *153*

**pumpkins**
Baked pumpkins *136*
Roasted pumpkin and sweet potato with
feta cheese *132*

*...Punch and Judy, saucy
postcards, fortune tellers and donkey
rides... 75*

## r

**raspberries**
Apple and raspberry tart *41*
Last summer fling crumble *47*
Midsummer cake *56*
Raspberry and mint sorbet *92*
Tipsy raspberries and cream *42*

relish, Tomato *68*
Rhubarb crumble *27*
rhubarb jellies, Orange and *26*
risotto, Chorizo and Savoy cabbage *172*

**rice**
Chorizo and Savoy cabbage risotto *172*
Green bean and herb rice *35*

**roast**
Roast beef salad *35*
Roast goose with chestnut and pancetta
stuffing *194*
Roast rib of beef *151*
Roasted potato wedges *104*
Roasted pumpkin and sweet potato with
feta cheese *132*
Roasted vegetables *105*

Rosé wine and strawberry jellies *114*

## s

**salads**
Asparagus, avocado and pea shoot
salad *14*
Chicken and avocado salad *34*
Chorizo and new potato salad *38*
Creamy potato salad *73*
Jersey Royal salad *16*
Lemon, chicken and spring onion
salad *34*
Pear, fig and Stichelton salad *103*
Red apple and Parma ham salad *37*
Roast beef salad *35*
Steak and goat's cheese salad *22*
Summer salad *53*
Warm bacon and scallop salad *86*
Warm chive potato salad *73*
Warm duck and red cabbage salad *174*
Watermelon, blueberry and mint salad *55*

**salmon**
Christmas morning breakfast *192*
Poached salmon with watercress and
chargrilled cherry tomatoes *83*
Smoked salmon, cream cheese and
cress wraps *61*

salsa, Cherry tomato and mint *52*
sandwich, Brie and bacon *127*

**sauces**
Cheese sauce for vegetables *106*
Feta cheese and watercress sauce *13*
Gravy *154*

**sausages**
Creamy sausage pasta *122*
Full English breakfast *146*
Sausage and lentil casserole *175*
Sausage and sweet potato mash *120*
Sausage baguettes with caramelised
onions *137*
Toad in the hole *162*

scallop salad, Warm bacon and *86*
scrambled duck eggs, Softly *19*
Scotch eggs *62*
sea bass with spinach and sautéed
potatoes, Baked *77*
*...shades of green woven into the
landscape... 59*

**shellfish**
crab parcels, Filo *84*
King prawn linguine *78*
Lobster *88*
Mussels in white wine *81*
Mussels with saffron and capellini *79*
scallop salad, Warm bacon and *86*

Shepherd's pie *163*
Slow lamb *160*
Slow roasted belly of pork *158*
Smoked salmon, cream cheese and
 cress wraps *61*
sorbet, Raspberry and mint *92*

**soups**
Bean and bacon soup *177*
Chestnut and smoky bacon soup *189*
Chilled cherry tomato and basil soup *50*
English Cheddar soup *121*
Spring vegetable soup *12*
Tomato and pasta soup with soured
 cream *125*

Spaghetti Bolognese *161*
Spaghetti with butter and parmesan
 cheese *127*

Spring vegetable soup *12*
Steak and goat's cheese salad *22*
Steak, Camembert and mushroom
 pancakes *101*
stew with dumplings, Beef and ale *183*
stock or broth, Chicken *156*

**strawberries**
Eton mess *53*
Last summer fling crumble *47*
Midsummer cake *56*
Rosé wine and strawberry jellies *114*
Strawberries with white balsamic
 vinegar *65*
Strawberry and clotted cream ice
 cream *92*
Strawberry chocolate meringues *112*

Summer berry ice cream *91*
Summer pavlova *43*
Summer salad *53*
swede mash, Carrot and *155*

# *t*

**tarts**
Apple and raspberry tart *41*
Chorizo and tomato tart *64*
Pear, blackberry and chocolate tart *129*

*...those first signs of life –
 the daffodils peeking through the
 ground, the green leaves forming on
 the trees, the singing of the new-born
 birds... 11*
Toad in the hole *162*
Toffee apples *139*

**tomatoes**
Cherry tomato and mint salsa *52*
Chicken, halloumi and cherry tomato

skewers *70*
Chilled cherry tomato and basil soup *50*
Full English breakfast *146*
Poached salmon with watercress and
 chargrilled cherry tomatoes *83*
Summer salad *53*
Tomato and pasta soup with soured
 cream *125*
Tomato relish *68*
Vegetable skewers *70*

trifle, Christmas *198*
trifle, Peaches and cream *42*
Turkey and cranberry parcels *193*

# *v*

Vanilla ice cream *91*
Vegetable skewers *70*
vegetables, Roasted *105*

**vegetarian**
Apple and raspberry tart *41*
Asparagus, avocado and pea shoot
 salad *14*
Asparagus, courgette and lemon pasta *25*
Baked apples *167*
Baked Camembert with asparagus
 dippers *23*
Baked potatoes *137*
Baked pumpkins *136*
Baked sweet potato *126*
Blueberry cheesecakes *108*
Caramelised orange puffs *110*
Carrot and swede mash *155*
Cashew nut brittle *186*
Cheese sauce for vegetables *106*
Cheese-smothered new potatoes *16*
Cheese straws *98*
Cheesy garlic bread *97*
Cheesy mash *179*
Cherry pie *44*
Cherry tomato and mint salsa *52*
Chilled cherry tomato and basil soup *50*
Christmas cookies *188*
Christmas pavlova *197*
Cinnamon hearts *28*
Creamy potato salad *73*
Crispy and fluffy roast potatoes *152*
Duck egg and chive omelette *17*
Duck egg chocolate cake *20*
Eggy bread *126*
English Cheddar soup *121*
Eton mess *53*
Fairy cakes *142*
Feta cheese and watercress sauce *13*
Fried duck eggs on toast *19*
Green bean and herb rice *35*
Halloween biscuits *135*
Home-made custard *166*
Home-made lemonade *32*
Honey and banana pancakes *169*

Honey peaches *114*
Iced orange wedges *58*
Jersey Royal salad *16*
Last summer fling crumble *47*
Leek omelette *176*
Marinated black olives *96*
Midsummer cake *56*
Orange and rhubarb jellies *26*
Peaches and cream trifle *42*
Pear, blackberry and chocolate tart *129*
Pear, fig and Stichelton salad *103*
Pimms and lemonade *58*
Plum crumble *165*
Pomegranate and passion fruit jellies *113*
Raspberry and mint sorbet *92*
Rhubarb crumble *27*
Roasted potato wedges *104*
Roasted pumpkin and sweet potato with
 feta cheese *132*
Roasted vegetables *105*
Rosé wine and strawberry jellies *114*
Softly scrambled duck eggs *19*
Spaghetti with butter and parmesan
 cheese *127*
Spring vegetable soup *12*
Strawberries with white balsamic
 vinegar *65*
Strawberry and clotted cream ice
 cream *92*
Strawberry chocolate meringues *112*
Summer pavlova *43*
The Parsons family coleslaw *72*
Tipsy raspberries and cream *42*
Toffee apples *139*
Tomato and pasta soup with soured
 cream *125*
Tomato relish *68*
Vanilla ice cream *91*
Warm chive potato salad *73*
Watermelon, blueberry and mint salad *55*

# *w*

*...walking through thick, powder-soft
 snow as it gently flutters down... 171*
watercress and chargrilled cherry
 tomatoes, Poached salmon with *83*
watercress sauce, Feta cheese and *13*
Watermelon, blueberry and mint salad *55*

**wine**
Chicken in lemon and white wine *107*
Lamb shanks braised in red wine *100*
Mussels in white wine *81*
Rosé wine and strawberry jellies *114*

# *y*

Yorkshire puddings *153*

# A note for American readers

British and American cookbooks use different measuring systems. In the UK, dry ingredients are measured by weight, with the metric system increasingly replacing the Imperial one, while in the US they are measured by volume.

| | |
|---|---|
| 7g | $^1/_4$ ounce |
| 20g | $^3/_4$ ounce |
| 25–30g | 1 ounce |
| 40g | $^1/_2$ ounces |
| 50g | $^3/_4$ ounces |
| 60–65g | $2^1/_4$ ounces |
| 70–75g | $2^1/_2$ ounces |
| 80g | $2^3/_4$ ounces |
| 90g | $3^1/_4$ ounces |
| 100g | $3^1/_2$ ounces |
| 110–115g | 4 ounces |
| 120–130g | $4^1/_2$ ounces |
| 140g | 5 ounces |
| 150g | $5^1/_2$ ounces |
| 175–180g | 6 ounces |
| 200g | 7 ounces |
| 220–225g | 8 ounces |
| 250–260g | 9 ounces |
| 300g | $10^1/_2$ ounces |
| 325g | $11^1/_2$ ounces |
| 350g | 12 ounces |
| 400g | 14 ounces |
| 450g | 1 pound |
| 500g | 1 pound 2 ounces |
| 600g | 1 pound 5 ounces |
| 700g | 1 pound 9 ounces |
| 750g | 1 pound 10 ounces |
| 800g | $1^3/_4$ pounds |
| 900g | 2 pounds |
| 1kg | $2^1/_4$ pounds |

| | |
|---|---|
| 50ml | $1^3/_4$ fl oz |
| 60ml | 2 fl oz (4 tablespoons/$^1/_4$ cup) |
| 75ml | $2^1/_2$ fl oz (5 tablespoons) |
| 90ml | 3 fl oz ($^3/_8$ cup) |
| 100ml | $3^1/_2$ fl oz |
| 125ml | 4 fl oz ($^1/_2$ cup) |
| 150ml | 5 fl oz ($^2/_3$ cup) |
| 175ml | 6 fl oz |
| 200ml | 7 fl oz |
| 250ml | 8 fl oz (1 cup) |
| 300ml | 10 fl oz |
| 350ml | 12 fl oz |
| 400ml | 14 fl oz |
| 450ml | 15 fl oz |
| 475ml | 16 fl oz (2 cups) |
| 500ml | 18 fl oz |
| 600ml | 20 fl oz |
| 800ml | 28 fl oz |
| 850ml | 30 fl oz |
| 1 litre | 35 fl oz (4 cups) |

| | |
|---|---|
| 5mm | $^1/_4$ inch |
| 1cm | $^1/_2$ inch |
| 2cm | $^3/_4$ inch |
| 2.5cm | 1 inch |
| 3cm | $1^1/_4$ inches |
| 4cm | $1^1/_2$ inches |
| 5cm | 2 inches |
| 6cm | $2^1/_2$ inches |
| 8cm | $3^1/_4$ inches |
| 9cm | $3^1/_2$ inches |
| 10cm | 4 inches |
| 12cm | $4^1/_2$ inches |
| 14cm | $5^1/_2$ inches |
| 20cm | 8 inches |
| 24cm | $9^1/_2$ inches |
| 30cm | 12 inches |

# Credits

Every effort has been made to credit the material illustrated and quoted from in this book. The publishers would like to apologise in advance for any ommisions and will seek to rectify those in future printings. All recipe photography in this book is the copyright of Cristian Barnett. The author photograph on page 207 was taken by Gene Weatherley and is used with permission. All family snapshots and some other uncredited images in this book courtesy of the author and/or the publisher. All other images (many of which have been digitally enhanced and reappear on other pages further to the ones listed here) are courtesy of Fotolia and copyright Fotolia/the following:

Page 5, red fabric background © Freesurf; page 14, recycled paper © Maria Adelaide Silva; page 28, background pink floral allover © Angela Cable; page 34, lettuce © hazel proudlove; pages 36-37, old photo 1 © Jumpingsack; pages 38-39 old wallpaper © clearviewstock; pages 44-45: vintage golde paper © Freesurf; page 46, grunge tag on white background © emily2k; pages 48-49, Red Poppy © Thomas Rehermann; page 58, grass © Peter Baxter; page 59, real picnic table cloth © klikk; page 65, Old Notebook © Stefanie Leuker; pages 74-75, dry pebbles © Robert Cocquyt; page 74, A sandcastle with a union jack flag on beach © russell witherington; page 74, two empty deckchairs on the sea front, st. ives, u © Sharpshot; page 74, punch puppet offering on stage copy-space © Steve Mann; page 74, Helter Skelter © Christopher Dodge; page 74, icecream © Sean Gladwell; page 74, a vintage blank irish postcard with a red stamp © Sharpshot; pages 78-79 horizon © Papo; pages 82-83, harvest moon over water © Gramper; pages 90-92, Abstract pattern © mordeccy; pages 94-95 [yellow flower], rio samba © Brenda Carson; pages 9 4-95 [white flower], Flower24 © Platinum Pictures; pages 94-95, The antique homespun linen cloth © alexcoolok; pages 100-101, grungy room © Phase4Photography; pages 110-111 pure perfection © Geoffrey Whiting; page 112, Torn Paper with Masking Tape © robynmac; pages 118-119, Drops of water © mashe; pages 120-121, feuilles d'automne © Tempo; page 122, Vintage floral background with old papers © Sandra Cunningham; pages 126-127, Abstract grunge red © Photosani; page 132, peeling paint © Paul Turner; page 140, Many pieces of puzzle © Vaclav Janousek; pages 140-141, rainy day © Heinrich; pages 144-145 [wood]: holz © Konstanze Gruber; pages 144-145, snow showers © Dianne McFadden; page 147, rust metallic surface © Dmitriy Chistoprudov; page 153 Cracked background © Cla78; pages 154-155, Baumstumpf © Konstanze Gruber; pages 156-157, smoke, swirls and art © Akhilesh Sharma; page 160, jahresringe © Konstanze Gruber; pages 164-165, alte papier © suzannmeer; page 167, three apples © Olga Lyubkin; pages 170-171, Steg im Nebel © Kerstin Selle; pages 174-175, Cracked wall © strixcode; pages 180-181, Frosty pattern © ELEN; page 184, Two glasses of a red wine with warm lights in the background © NinaMalyna; pages 192-193, red berries from a holly tree © Vaide Seskauskiene; page 199, Fußspuren auf verschneiter Straße © Ingo Zimmermann; pages 200-205, Old paper isolated on white © Viktor Pravdica; pages 206-207, Old Notebook © Stefanie Leuker; page 207, summer flower, buttercup, spearwort © Patrick Hermans; page 207, dandelion © Tomasz Plawski; page 207, Running down puddles © pressmaster; page 207, early mass-produced personal computer from 1980 © rudybaby; page 207, Dough © Lasse Kristensen;

Excerpts acknowledged from the following: *Wuthering Heights*, Emily Bronte (page 32); *Wind in the Willows*, Kenneth Grahame (page 60); *Dover Beach*, Matthew Arnold (page 82); *Winnie the Pooh*, A.A. Milne (page 112); *Autumn Days*, Estelle White (page 118); *Let It Snow*, Sammy Cahn (page 170); *The Christmas Song*, Mel Tormé and Robert Wells (page 189); *A Christmas Carol*, Charles Dickens (page 190).

The recipe on page 136 is adapted from an original recipe by Hugh Fearnley-Whittingstall.

# Some things about *me*

**I used to hold buttercups** under the chins of my friends; blow dandelions into the breeze; jump in puddles and make big splashes. I liked to sip fizzy lemonade through straws and feel the bubbles on my tongue. I looked in wonder at rainbows and dreamed about finding the end of one.

Then I grew up… and got to play house for real. I bought some cookbooks and taught myself how to make nice meals for my friends and family.

I *loved* cooking: never happier than when my hands were sticky with dough and there was flour in my hair and the scent of vanilla sugar under my nose.

In 2006, I discovered blogging. I set up my own blog where I jotted down some thoughts about food. I called it *A Slice of Cherry Pie*. People started to read the blog and I read theirs and a kind of community grew. In 2007, I tried to put a roof over all our heads by founding the UK Food Bloggers Association.

I carried on writing and creating recipes. *The Times* included my blog in their list of the world's fifty best food blogs.

In 2008 I found a literary agent. They found a publisher and together we created a cookbook… …and **found the end** of one of those rainbows that I dreamed about when I was a little girl.

# Thank you

There are many people to thank for this book and for helping to make my dream of it a reality.

First and foremost I want to thank my mum and my husband, Rob, for their unconditional love and unwavering belief in me, especially at those times when I needed it the most. I love you more than words can say.

To my family and friends, thank you for your support, enthusiasm and encouragement, and for your understanding during those busy times when you saw less of me. I am truly blessed to have you.

I am so very fortunate to have been given this opportunity by Jon Croft and Meg Avent at Absolute Press, and to have had the pleasure of working with such a great team. Thank you all so very much.

I am eternally grateful to Matt Inwood, the Art Director at Absolute Press, who has been so in tune with my vision for this book and who has made it everything I dreamt of and more. I couldn't have wished for a more talented designer, or for one who would take the hand of an inexperienced author and lead her through the entire publishing process, making it such fun along the way. Matt, you are one in a million.

Many thanks to Claire Siggery for the inspired cover design and work on the beautiful pages within.

Thank you to Andrea O'Connor who styled the food so beautifully and to Cristian Barnett, who captured it through his lens so artfully, giving it such life.
Thank you also to Jane Bamforth who provided invaluable guidance and suggestions as she polished my recipes.

To the very lovely Elizabeth of Mar, thank you for letting the world know about this book through your work in publicising it.

To everyone at Limelight Management, but especially to Mary, thank you for taking me under your wing.

A very big thank you must go to everyone who helped me to test the recipes, whether by cooking or by tasting. Special thanks in particular to Vanessa Johnson, Amanda Matthews, Dan Morgan, Kelly Morgan, Carol Parsons, John Parsons, Alan Ransome, Linda Snellin, Nicole Snellin, Doris Tickner and Malcolm Witcher.

I am indebted to the many food writers and chefs who have given me such inspiration and, through their words, have been my mentors in the kitchen. The list is long but I must mention Hugh Fearnley-Whittingstall, Nigella Lawson, Jamie Oliver, Nigel Slater and Rick Stein.

Finally I want to thank, from the bottom of my heart, every single reader of my blog over the years, everyone who has taken the time and trouble to comment on my posts or send me an email, and the friends I have made through the wonderful food blogging community to which I belong. It is each of you who has given me the encouragement to write and to develop my recipes and who helped me to believe that, just perhaps, I could write a cookbook. Thank you for coming on this journey with me; it wouldn't have been possible without you.